THE
COAST TO COAST
WALK

190 miles across Northern England

Yorkshire Dales
National Park

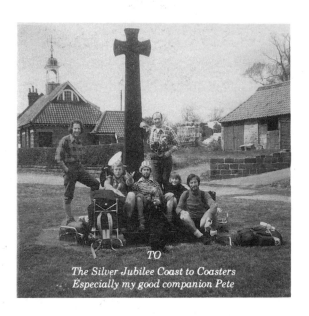

TO

The Silver Jubilee Coast to Coasters
Especially my good companion Pete

THE
COAST TO COAST
WALK

190 miles across Northern England

by

Paul Hannon

HILLSIDE PUBLICATIONS

HILLSIDE PUBLICATIONS
11 Nessfield Grove
Exley Head
Keighley
West Yorkshire
BD22 6NU

First published 1992
© Paul Hannon 1992

*The maps in this book are based upon
the 1900-1930 Ordnance Survey 1:10,560 maps*

ISBN 1 870141 18 0

Printed in Great Britain by:
Carnmor Print and Design
95/97 London Road
Preston
Lancashire
PR1 4BA

CONTENTS

St Bees Head

Robin Hood's Bay

INTRODUCTION

Coast to Coast - the very name is inspiring, from clifftop to clifftop across our small but perfectly formed land, magnificent strides through some of the grandest scenery in the North. The mountains of Lakeland, the Pennine uplands, glorious Swaledale, the Cleveland Hills, and Eskdale and the North York Moors, so much magic in so little space! Little wonder that walkers relish its clarion call, and enthuse ever afterwards over its finest moments.

As originator of the Coast to Coast Walk in the early 1970s, the late A.Wainwright was a hallowed name to tens of thousands of hillwalkers through his previous guidebooks, but the media subsequently transformed him into a household name, and the end result is that few people have not now heard of the Coast to Coast Walk. Having devised the entire route himself through his personal cross-section of the North's best walking country, it may be regarded as his finest hour, and as such is just that little bit special.

It gives particular satisfaction to a long-standing admirer of the walk's creator to bring it into the 1990s - this volume is indeed a personal tribute to Wainwright, a more practical memorial than a cairn or a re-named tarn. In his glory days Wainwright was never less than a perfectionist, and if this guide falls short of his exacting standards, he would surely have been happy to see his followers on the right track.

This book takes on board the many changes that have occurred in two decades, from inevitable ones such as hedges being ripped up, and new stiles and waymarking, to changes brought about by path diversions, permissive path creations, or simply to accommodate the wishes of landowners. Various suggestions for local alternatives on rights of way are included, though the guide adheres to the original route where it remains in common use. Only on a couple of occasions have I introduced the walk to logically sited footpaths to avoid unnecessary and potentially dangerous road walking.

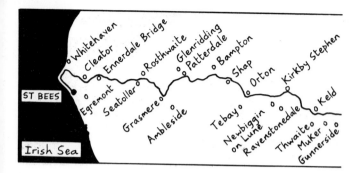

Despite the walk's longevity there remain some contentious sections that do not follow currently defined rights of way. Though these generally cover open moor or fell, problems have arisen both for nature conservation and landowners due to the large numbers of walkers. Certain sections, therefore - notably between Shap and Keld - are undergoing re-routing negotiations, so it is especially important that walkers show a sensitive respect for their surroundings, and are prepared to heed the advice of any diversion notices that might appear after the book's publication. New changes to the route will be incorporated in future editions.

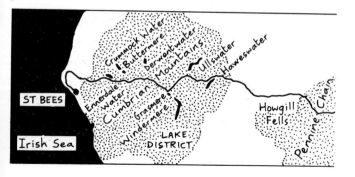

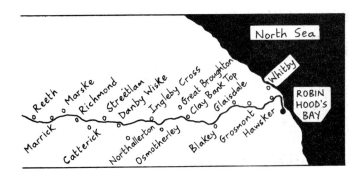

Reeth Marske Richmond Streetlam Danby Wiske Ingleby Cross Great Broughton Clay Bank Top Glaisdale

Marrick Catterick Northallerton Osmotherley Blakey Grosmont Hawsker

Whitby

North Sea

ROBIN HOOD'S BAY

Grosmont Bridge

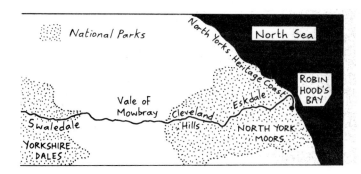

National Parks

North Yorks Heritage Coast

North Sea

ROBIN HOOD'S BAY

Vale of Mowbray

Swaledale

Cleveland Hills

Eskdale

YORKSHIRE DALES

NORTH YORK MOORS

The Coast to Coast Walk runs from St Bees on the Cumbrian coast to Robin Hood's Bay on the Yorkshire coast, a distance of 190 miles. Within these pages the walk has been divided into twelve different stages for practical purposes, but as the sketch maps and mileages are continuous, this will have little effect on each individual's chosen route. Most people will be aiming to complete the walk within a two-week period, which would normally allow fourteen overnights.

Thanks to the growing number of establishments catering for Coast to Coast walkers (particularly welcome in areas outside the National Parks) any number of permutations can be devised to suit one's needs. Unless planning to come out of season it is vital to book in advance to ensure a bed at the end of each day. Campers are particularly well catered for, on the whole, and are more likely to get by on a casual day to day basis.

Access to the start and finish of the route is not too difficult. St Bees is on a British Rail line, and its station connects with Carlisle (north) and Barrow, for Lancaster (south). Robin Hood's Bay long since lost its station, but is served by the Whitby-Scarborough bus which links with railway stations in both towns. Certainly if heading south then the longer bus ride to Scarborough will find one with a better service to the main line at York.

The unexpected popularity of the walk has led to a cottage industry in the provision of accommodation lists, which now sell in their own right as little booklets. The reason for their great value is the fact that the walk travels through many different districts, and collating all the necessary information can be a complicated affair. These booklets can be found in some shops, or obtained from the sources listed   (Ring first for availability and prices.)

Mrs. Whitehead
East Stonesdale Farm
Keld, Richmond
North Yorkshire
DL11 6LJ
Tel: 0748-86374

North York Moors
  Adventure Centre
Park House, Ingleby Cross
Northallerton,
North Yorkshire
DL6 3PE
Tel: 0609-82571

Leading Edge Press & Publishing,
The Old Chapel,
Burtersett, Hawes,
North Yorkshire DL8 3PB
Tel: 0969-667566
(a larger book, which includes listings for several other long-distance walks in the North of England)

Two further services have recently been created specifically for Coast to Coast walkers. The first is a backpack shuttle service which will transport your groaning rucksack onto your evening's objective: for further details contact the Coast to Coast Packhorse (05396-23688), or Kirkby Stephen Information Centre. The other is a minibus service linking Robin Hood's Bay with Kirkby Stephen station, by way of Northallerton's main-line station. This is operated by In Step, 35 Cokeham Road, Lancing, West Sussex (0903-766475). In either case, continuing operations will depend upon levels of usage.

Finally, bear in mind that coffee table books and television portray only the glamorous side of a long-distance walk, giving little mention of blood, sweat and tears. Weather (incessant rain, or, believe it or not, heatwaves), blisters, or simply a heavy pack day after day can all contribute to a sad experience. Seasoned hillwalkers should have little difficulty in taking the Coast to Coast Walk in their stride, but the less experienced should ensure they become 'more' experienced before venturing on a multi-day trek such as this: the Northern Hills are much in evidence!

In practise the twelve sections form a reasonable basis, with some useful variations listed below. (Route alternatives within each section are included in their respective introduction.)

1) If not leaving St Bees first thing, re-adjust the first two days by halting before Ennerdale: it still shouldn't be too far to Rosthwaite on Day 2.

2) Break up Day 3 with an overnight at Grasmere, permitting a more adventurous walk the second day, or simply time to sample Grasmere.

3) Break up Day 5 at either Orton (too early if starting from Shap, but useful if starting from Bampton) or the Newbiggin on Lune area in place of Kirkby Stephen - this splits Days 5 and 6 more evenly.

4) Anyone wishing to save a day could merge Days 6, 7 and 8 into two, by taking the valley route rather than the moors route through Swaledale, in which case several villages offer a break.

5) As Day 8 is such a short stage, continue it to Catterick Bridge. If wishing to sample Richmond, return to it by bus and catch it back out to Catterick Bridge in the morning. Alternatively, simply break up Day 9 at any of several locations, allowing a later departure from Richmond.

6) Extend the final three days into four by substituting Glaisdale with Blakey and Grosmont. This is a little uneven though, as Clay Bank Top to Blakey will probably be deemed too short, and in any case the miles do continue very easily to Glaisdale. However, if descending into Farndale for the 'Blakey' overnight, then it might seem enough of a day. If keeping to three days from Ingleby Cross to the sea, an alternative is simply to replace Clay Bank Top with Blakey (a longer day), and Glaisdale with Grosmont (two shorter days).

7) If aiming for a same day getaway from Robin Hood's Bay, break the final day at Hawsker for a lunchtime finish at Robin Hood's Bay.

ORDNANCE SURVEY MAPS

The following 1:50,000 Landranger sheets cover the route, giving a complete picture of the neighbourhood of the walk, and the location of alternative routes and other features.

89 West Cumbria
90 Penrith, Keswick & Ambleside
91 Appleby in Westmorland
92 Barnard Castle
93 Middlesbrough & Darlington
94 Whitby
98 Wensleydale & Upper Wharfedale
99 Northallerton & Ripon

Hasty Bank from the climb to Urra Moor

THE COUNTRY CODE

* Respect the life and work of the countryside
* Protect wildlife, plants and trees
* Keep to public paths across farmland
* Safeguard water supplies
* Go carefully on country roads
* Keep dogs under control
* Guard against all risks of fire
* Fasten all gates
* Leave no litter - take it with you
* Make no unnecessary noise
* Leave livestock, crops and machinery alone
* Use gates and stiles to cross fences, hedges and walls

SOME USEFUL FACILITIES
A general guide only

	Youth Hostel	Accommodation	Camping	Inn	Bus Service	Rail Station	Post Office	Other Shop	WC	Payphone
St Bees		*	*	*	*	*	*	*	*	*
Sandwith		*		*			*			*
Moor Row		*					*			*
Cleator		*		*	*		*	*		*
Ennerdale Bridge		*	*	*			*			*
Gillerthwaite	*		*							*
Black Sail Hut	*									
Honister Pass	*									
Seatoller		*	*		*			*	*	*
Rosthwaite	*	*	*	*	*		*		*	*
Stonethwaite		*	*	*			*			*
Grasmere	*	*		*	*		*	*	*	*
Glenridding	*	*	*	*	*		*	*	*	*
Patterdale	*	*	*	*	*		*	*	*	*
Burnbanks										*
Bampton		*	*	*			*			*
Rosgill										*
Shap		*	*	*	*		*	*	*	*
Oddendale		*								
Orton		*		*	*		*			*
Tebay	*	*		*	*		*			*
Raisbeck		*			*					*
Newbiggin on Lune		*	*		*					*
Ravenstonedale		*	*	*	*		*			*
Kirkby Stephen	*	*	*	*	*	*	*	*	*	*
Hartley										*
Keld	*	*	*		*				*	*
Muker		*	*	*	*		*	*	*	*
Gunnerside		*		*	*		*	*	*	*
Low Row		*		*	*				*	*
Healaugh					*					*
Reeth		*	*	*	*		*	*	*	*
Grinton	*	*		*	*		*		*	*

	Youth Hostel	Accommodation	Camping	Inn	Bus Service	Rail Station	Post Office	Other Shop	WC	Payphone
Marrick		*								*
Marske		*								*
Richmond		*	*	*	*		*	*	*	*
Colburn				*	*		*	*		*
Brompton on Swale		*	*	*	*		*			*
Catterick Bridge		*	*	*	*					*
Scorton				*	*		*	*		*
Bolton on Swale		*	*							*
Whitwell		*								
Streetlam		*								*
Danby Wiske		*	*	*						*
Oaktree Hill		*	*		*					*
East Harlsey				*	*		*			*
Ingleby Arncliffe		*			*					
Ingleby Cross		*	*	*	*		*			*
Osmotherley	*	*		*	*		*	*	*	*
Swainby				*	*		*		*	*
Huthwaite Green										*
Carlton Bank								*	*	*
Carlton		*		*	*		*			*
Cringle Moor		*	*							
Great Broughton		*	*	*	*		*	*		*
Chop Gate		*		*	*				*	*
Blakey		*	*	*						
Glaisdale		*	*	*		*	*	*	*	*
Egton Bridge		*		*		*			*	*
Grosmont		*		*	*	*	*	*	*	*
Sleights		*		*	*	*	*	*	*	*
Littlebeck		*	*							*
Hawsker		*	*	*	*		*			*
Robin Hood's Bay	*	*	*	*	*		*	*	*	*

SOME USEFUL ADDRESSES

Organisations
Ramblers' Association
1/5 Wandsworth Road, London SW8 2XX
Tel: 071-582 6878

Youth Hostels Association
Lakeland Regional Office, Barclays Bank Chambers,
Crescent Road, Windermere, Cumbria LA23 1EA
Tel: 05394-42301
Northern Regional Office, D Floor, Milburn House, Dean Street,
Newcastle-upon-Tyne NE1 1LF
Tel: 091-221 2101

Friends of the Lake District
No.3, Yard 77, Highgate, Kendal, Cumbria LA9 4ED
Tel: 0539-720788

Yorkshire Dales Society
Otley Civic Centre, Cross Green, Otley,
West Yorkshire LS21 1HD
Tel: 0943-607868

Information - Tourist Boards, National Parks
Cumbria Tourist Board
Ashleigh, Holly Road, Windermere, Cumbria LA23 2AQ
Tel: 05394-44444

Yorkshire & Humberside Tourist Board
312 Tadcaster Road, York YO2 2HF
Tel: 0904-707961

Lake District National Park Visitor Services
Brockhole, Windermere, Cumbria LA23 1LJ
Tel: 05394-46601

Yorkshire Dales National Park Information
Colvend, Hebden Road, Grassington, Skipton,
North Yorkshire BD23 5LB
Tel: 0756-752748

North York Moors National Park Information Service
The Old Vicarage, Bondgate, Helmsley, York YO6 5BP
Tel: 0439-70657

Information - on or near the walk
Whitehaven Tourist Information
Civic Centre, Lowther Street, Whitehaven, Cumbria CA28 7DG
Tel: 0946-695678

Egremont Tourist Information
12 Main Street, Egremont, Cumbria CA22 2DW
Tel: 0946-820693

Seatoller National Park Information
Seatoller Barn, Seatoller, Keswick, Cumbria CA12 5XN
Tel: 059684-294

Grasmere National Park Information
Redbank Road, Grasmere, Ambleside, Cumbria LA22 9SW
Tel: 05394-35245

Glenridding National Park Information
Car park, Glenridding, Penrith, Cumbria
Tel: 08532-414

Kirkby Stephen Tourist Information
Market Square, Kirkby Stephen, Cumbria CA17 4QN
Tel: 07683-71199

Reeth Tourist Information
Swaledale Folk Museum, Reeth Green, Reeth, Richmond,
North Yorkshire DL11 6QT
Tel: 0748-84517

Richmond Tourist Information
Friary Gardens, Victoria Road, Richmond,
North Yorkshire DL10 4AJ
Tel: 0748-850252

Northallerton Tourist Information
The Applegarth, Northallerton, North Yorkshire DL7 8LZ
Tel: 0609-776864

The Moors Centre, Danby, Whitby, North Yorkshire YO21 2NB
Tel: 0287-660654

Whitby Tourist Information
New Quay Road, Whitby, North Yorkshire YO21 1DH
Tel: 0947-602674

Major Bus Operators
Cumberland Motor Services
Tangier Street, Whitehaven, Cumbria
Tel: 0946-63222

United Automobile Services
Grange Road, Darlington, Co. Durham DL1 5NL
Tel: 0325-468771

Tees & District Transport Company
Newport Road Bus Station, Middlesbrough, Cleveland TS1 5AH
Tel: 0642-210131

Scarborough & District Motor Services
Valley Bridge Garage, Scarborough, North Yorkshire
Tel: 0723-375463

THE ROUTE GUIDE

The main body of this book is a detailed guide to the walk itself, extending from page 20 to page 139. It is divided into twelve sections, each having its own introduction: these are quickly located by reference to the contents on page 5. Each introduction includes a gradient profile of the route (vertical scale greatly exaggerated) and a summary of the walking, along with suggestions for alternatives to the main route. Many are the result of personal exploration, and can all be plotted from the Landranger maps.

A continuous strip-map runs throughout the guide, accompanied by a narrative of the route. Remaining space is then devoted to notes and illustrations of features of interest along the way.

Key to the map symbols

19

SECTION 1
ST BEES TO ENNERDALE BRIDGE

14 miles   *1900 feet of ascent*

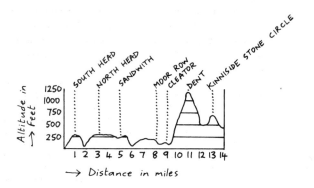

The opening day offers three well-defined sections, though in this sandwich the filling is the least appetising part. That rare creature the Cumbrian clifftop provides an inspiring introduction to the walk, several airy miles of tall sea cliffs putting one in the perfect frame of mind for a near-200-mile walk. On leaving the coast there follow several miles that are interesting but unexciting, as a corner of the ill-fated West Cumberland industrial belt is traversed. Ahead, however, are the hills, and beyond Cleator the unassuming little fell of Dent, is, despite afforestation, a foretaste of Lakeland.

Alternatives, other than short-cuts, are few: this is a more circuitous day than most, and an obvious bee-line for Ennerdale Bridge can be plotted. Other than a path climbing from St Bees to Loughrigg Farm, however, road walking dominates the short-cut. The two great natural features of the walk are both time-consuming, though only in desperation should St Bees Head be omitted: there's nothing like it for a long time! If flagging, the back road from Cleator to Ennerdale Bridge avoids Dent.

When the great moment arrives, and you're stood on the sea wall facing the Irish Sea, ensure the first task is completed by dipping at least a toe into its waters before heading for the cliffs. The sea wall ends abruptly where a footbridge crosses Rottington Beck and a sign points to St Bees Head and Fleswick Bay. Additional signs advise of the presence of an RSPB nature reserve and dangerous cliffs, both of significance. Ascent to the clifftops is by way of a steep flight of wooden steps, after which it's easy going up aloft for an inspiring introduction to the Coast to Coast Walk. A clear day carries the immediate bonus of extensive views inland to the mountains of Wasdale.

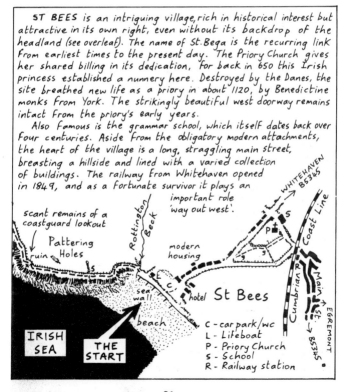

ST BEES is an intriguing village, rich in historical interest but attractive in its own right, even without its backdrop of the headland (see overleaf). The name of St.Bega is the recurring link from earliest times to the present day. The Priory Church gives her shared billing in its dedication, for back in 650 this Irish princess established a nunnery here. Destroyed by the Danes, the site breathed new life as a priory in about 1120, by Benedictine monks from York. The strikingly beautiful west doorway remains intact from the priory's early years.

Also famous is the grammar school, which itself dates back over four centuries. Aside from the obligatory modern attachments, the heart of the village is a long, straggling main street, breasting a hillside and lined with a varied collection of buildings. The railway from Whitehaven opened in 1849, and as a fortunate survivor it plays an important role 'way out west'.

WHITEHAVEN B5345

Cumbrian Coast Line

scant remains of a coastguard lookout

Pattering Holes

ruin

Rottington Beck

modern housing

Main St.

EGREMONT B5345

sea wall

hotel St Bees

beach

IRISH SEA

THE START

C - car park/wc
L - Lifeboat
P - Priory Church
S - School
R - Railway station

21

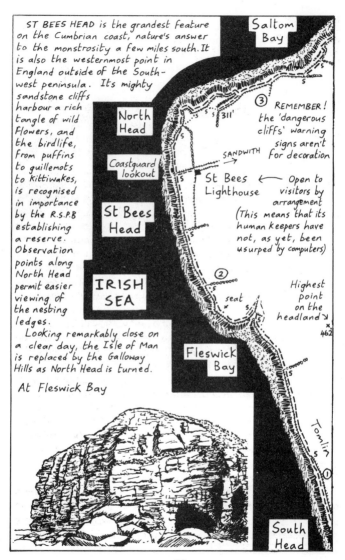

ST BEES HEAD is the grandest feature on the Cumbrian coast, nature's answer to the monstrosity a few miles south. It is also the westernmost point in England outside of the South-west peninsula. Its mighty sandstone cliffs harbour a rich tangle of wild flowers, and the birdlife, from puffins to guillemots to kittiwakes, is recognised in importance by the R.S.P.B establishing a reserve. Observation points along North Head permit easier viewing of the nesting ledges.

Looking remarkably close on a clear day, the Isle of Man is replaced by the Galloway Hills as North Head is turned.

At Fleswick Bay

Saltom Bay

North Head

Coastguard lookout

St Bees Head

IRISH SEA

③ REMEMBER! the 'dangerous cliffs' warning signs aren't for decoration

SANDWITH →

St Bees Lighthouse ← Open to visitors by arrangement (This means that its human keepers have not, as yet, been usurped by computers)

311'

② seat ×

Highest point on the headland ↓ × 462

Fleswick Bay

Tomlin

①

South Head

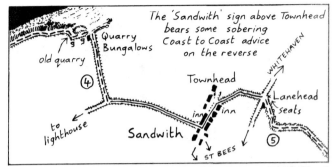

The 'Sandwith' sign above Townhead bears some sobering Coast to Coast advice on the reverse

old quarry

Quarry Bungalows

to lighthouse

Sandwith

Townhead

inn   inn

↓ ST BEES

WHITEHAVEN

Lanehead seats

④

⑤

After a long time on the seaward side of the fence on South Head, the path transfers over for a steady drop to the prominent inlet of Fleswick Bay. The path descends to within a few feet of sea level before regaining height for the longer march atop North Head, though many will be tempted to venture onto the shore. Here are cliffs, flowers, birds, caves, water-worn rocks, and a dazzling array of smooth pebbles underfoot - and of course the sea. The path can be regained by locating a series of holds in the rock to a hurdle above, avoiding having to go inland to the main stile.

Forging on below the lighthouse and alongside the lookout the path is soon returned in dramatic fashion to the clifftop around the point of North Head. Ahead Saltom Bay laps the Whitehaven shoreline, with the harbour entrance visible to the discerning eye. An easier route stays on the land side of the fence, crossing to a stile to meet the more entertaining main path. The main path descends, surprisingly, appearing to lead out onto a limb: in fact it passes below a detached inland cliff and a 'hidden' green pasture, before a little clamber up through the sandstone to the top path. Remaining largely on the seaward side now, the end of the cliff walk comes as a shock on emerging above the former Birkhams Quarry, a right mess!

At the cottages turn inland on a rough lane sunken between hedgerows, then turn left at a junction with the lighthouse road to enter Sandwith. Turn left in the village, curving up to the right past the *Dog & Partridge* to a junction at Lanehead. Cross straight over to run the full length of a gem of a green byway.

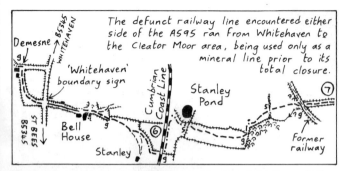

The defunct railway line encountered either side of the A595 ran from Whitehaven to the Cleator Moor area, being used only as a mineral line prior to its total closure.

The byway runs along to Demesne, turning right through the farmyard and out along a rough track onto the B5345 Whitehaven-St Bees road. Cross straight over and along the farm road to Bell House. Keep on past it to a gateway on a brow with a splendid prospect ahead, beyond the circular Stanley Pond and the railway line. As the track forks on descent, bear right to a gate, then soon trend left down a thinner branch towards another gate, but keeping on down the field-side to a railway underpass. On the other side go left to the shrubbery enclosing Stanley Pond, and seek out a stile in the hedge on the right. A path runs through a long enclosure towards a wood, escaping by a gate on the left before swinging right to climb through two fields to another railway underpass. An enclosed track then climbs up to meet the busy A595 Whitehaven-Egremont road. After a last look back to the St Bees coast, cross with care and go straight along the unglamorous Scalegill Road to enter Moor Row. It bears left past the war memorial to a junction by the village shop, and here turn right to quickly leave the village.

Over a brow the leafy lane is also vacated by a stile on the left, and after rising to a brow, a field-path soon slants across to another ripped-up mineral line, thence continuing clearly on towards Cleator, directly ahead. With a well-tended cricket ground in front, the path joins the head of a lane to enter Cleator's main street. Go left a short way to a shop in a terrace, and turn down Kiln Brow opposite. At the bottom go right at a housing development to Blackhow Bridge over the Ehen, from where a rough byway climbs away.

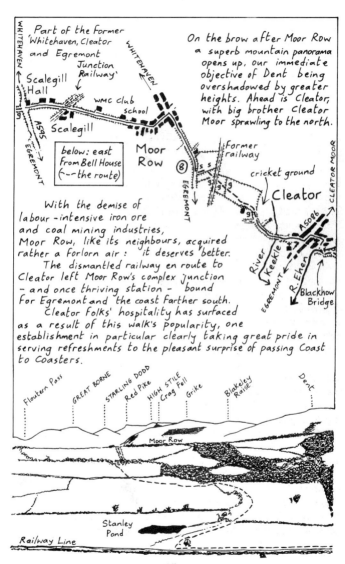

Part of the former 'Whitehaven, Cleator and Egremont Junction Railway'

WHITEHAVEN ↑

Scalegill Hall

A595

EGREMONT ↓

WHITEHAVEN

Scalegill

WMC club

school

below: east from Bell House (--the route)

Moor Row

⑧

s s

EGREMONT ↓

Former railway

s s

g

cricket ground

Cleator

g

CLEATOR MOOR →

A5086

River Keekle

R Ehen

R EGREMONT

Blackhow Bridge

On the brow after Moor Row a superb mountain panorama opens up, our immediate objective of Dent being overshadowed by greater heights. Ahead is Cleator, with big brother Cleator Moor sprawling to the north.

With the demise of labour-intensive iron ore and coal mining industries, Moor Row, like its neighbours, acquired rather a forlorn air: it deserves better.

The dismantled railway en route to Cleator left Moor Row's complex junction – and once thriving station – bound for Egremont and the coast farther south.

Cleator folks' hospitality has surfaced as a result of this walk's popularity, one establishment in particular clearly taking great pride in serving refreshments to the pleasant surprise of passing Coast to Coasters.

Floutern Pass · GREAT BORNE · STARLING DODD · Red Pike · HIGH STILE Crag Fell · Grike · Blakeley Raise · Dent

Moor Row

Stanley Pond

Railway Line

25

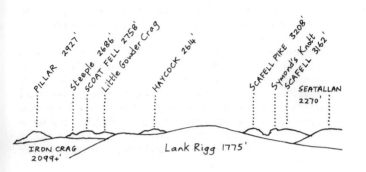

PILLAR 2927'

Steeple 2686'
SCOAT FELL 2758'
Little Gowder Crag

HAYCOCK 2614'

SCAFELL PIKE 3208'
Symond's Knott
SCAFELL 3162'

SEATALLAN 2270'

IRON CRAG 2099+'

Lank Rigg 1775'

Looking east to the Lakeland Fells from Dent

The Scafell peaks are 11 miles distant

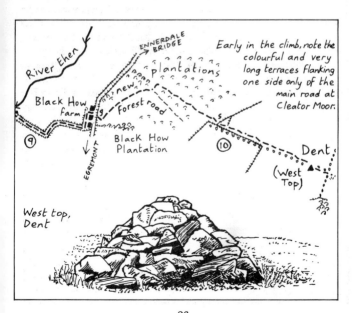

River Ehen

ENNERDALE BRIDGE

plantations

Early in the climb, note the colourful and very long terraces flanking one side only of the main road at Cleator Moor.

Black How farm

new

Forest road

Black How Plantation

EGREMONT

9

10

Dent
(West Top)

West top, Dent

First stage of the ascent of Dent, the lane works up the slope to Black How Farm, passing round the nearside of the buildings to emerge on a road.

The gate opposite gives access to the open fell, which is becoming less open as new plantations conspire to bury the flanks without trace. A standard-issue forest road doubles back up to the left with far-reaching views over the West Cumberland plain. When some height has been gained a sign sends a path a few yards off to the left to resume a parallel climb on a more accommodating surface. The pleasant path soon breaks free of the plantations, maintaining its straight line to arrive at the big cairn atop Dent.

This is only the traditional summit and not the true one, which is found across the marshy depression to the east. Though possessing the most diminutive of cairns, the highest point claims the distinct advantage of turning its back on the plain in favour of its grandstand setting for Lakeland's western skyline, at the heart of which is the deep enclave of Ennerdale to be penetrated on the next stage of the journey. This wilderness panorama stretches from Hopegill Head through Grasmoor, High Stile, Pillar and the Scafells to the Black Combe ridge.

Descend to a stile in a forest fence, quickly entering trees to run down a broad track to a junction: bear left along the forest road, but as it turns to drop away, take with relish a stile in the fence ahead, to gain a breath of fresh air on the contrastingly open eastern shoulder of the fell. A clear path runs to the far end to drop uncomfortably steeply to Nannycatch Beck. Turn left on the path through this narrow and immensely pleasant little valley, over a brace of footbridges and a stile at Nannycatch Gate.

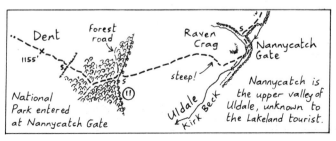

Passing below Flatfell Screes up to the left, the path and beck fade, and here bear right to work steadily up to the open fell road. A newer path emerges beyond Kinniside Stone Circle, which well merits an inspection. Go left along the road for a steady descent to Ennerdale Bridge, enjoying the parade of mountains as a finale to this stage. At the bottom turn right for the village.

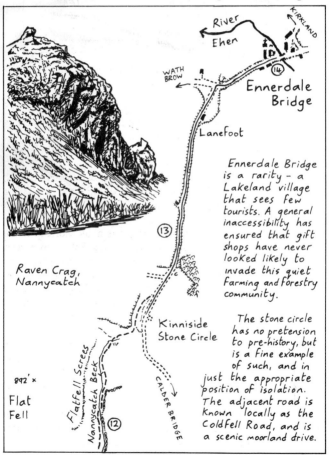

KIRKLAND

River Ehen

WATH BROW

Ennerdale Bridge

(14)

Lanefoot

(13)

Raven Crag, Nannycatch

Kinniside Stone Circle

Flatfell Screes

Nannycatch Beck

CALDER BRIDGE

892' x

Flat Fell

(12)

Ennerdale Bridge is a rarity - a Lakeland village that sees few tourists. A general inaccessibility has ensured that gift shops have never looked likely to invade this quiet farming and forestry community.

The stone circle has no pretension to pre-history, but is a fine example of such, and in just the appropriate position of isolation. The adjacent road is known locally as the Coldfell Road, and is a scenic moorland drive.

28

SECTION 2

ENNERDALE BRIDGE TO ROSTHWAITE

14 ¹/₂ miles

1800 feet of ascent

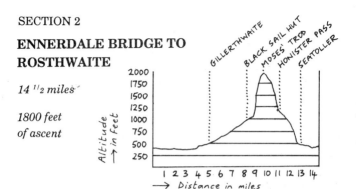

Another triple-section day comprising lakeshore, forest and mountainside as a tramp along the length of Ennerdale precedes a crossing into the head of Borrowdale. The opening miles are a splendid ramble along the southern shore of Ennerdale Water. While the higher reaches of the dale are draped in forestry, progress is rapid on a track giving glimpses up to the surrounding fells. Beyond Black Sail Hut the open air might have come off a prescription as, faced by high mountains, the inevitable climb brings fresh views and a varied descent into Borrowdale.

There are no shorter alternatives, but a plethora of more adventurous routes. These all involve serious fellwalking, and are best left to the strong and experienced, particularly at such an early stage of a long walk. In any case, they should only be tackled on a clear day. Least arduous fellwalking alternative leaves the valley for Scarth Gap, and from the pass a well-worn path climbs to the summit of Haystacks, continuing on less obvious paths to Moses' Trod. This route takes on a certain poignancy in view of the great man's final resting place. Higher level options include the High Stile ridge to the north, signposted from Gillerthwaite; and an ascent of Great Gable from the dalehead, continuing north to Moses' Trod or descending to Seathwaite.

Variations near the outset would be to use the north shore path and forest road to the head of the lake; and the forest road south of the river as far as the Pillar footbridge.

Leave the village by the Croasdale Road, turning right for the lake where indicated on a zigzag road that expires upon crossing the river Ehen. Go left past the pumping station on a broad track to the foot of Ennerdale Water, there turning right along the south shore footpath. This runs undeviatingly along the length of the lake, always within yards of the water's edge. High up to the right in the early stages the fangs of Crag Fell Pinnacles tower menacingly above, while the individual highlight is the scrambly crossing of the base of Anglers' Crag, which plummets directly into the water.

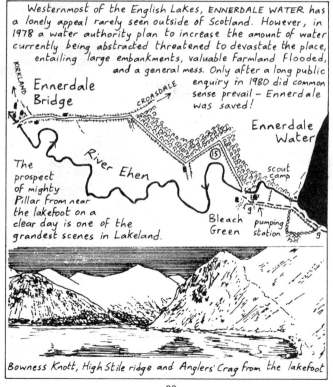

Westernmost of the English Lakes, ENNERDALE WATER has a lonely appeal rarely seen outside of Scotland. However, in 1978 a water authority plan to increase the amount of water currently being abstracted threatened to devastate the place, entailing large embankments, valuable farmland flooded, and a general mess. Only after a long public enquiry in 1980 did common sense prevail – Ennerdale was saved!

KIRKLAND

Ennerdale Bridge

CROASDALE

Ennerdale Water

River Ehen

15

scout camp

The prospect of mighty Pillar from near the lakefoot on a clear day is one of the grandest scenes in Lakeland.

Bleach Green

pumping station

g

g

Bowness Knott, High Stile ridge and Anglers' Crag from the lakefoot

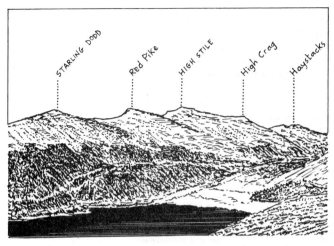

The high mountain wall enclosing the north side of
Ennerdale, seen from the slopes of Crag Fell, above our path

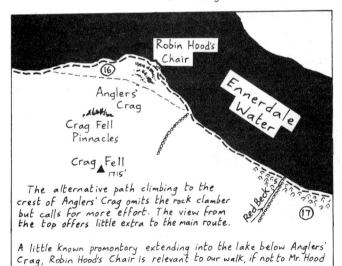

The alternative path climbing to the
crest of Anglers' Crag omits the rock clamber
but calls for more effort. The view from
the top offers little extra to the main route.

A little known promontory extending into the lake below Anglers'
Crag, Robin Hood's Chair is relevant to our walk, if not to Mr. Hood

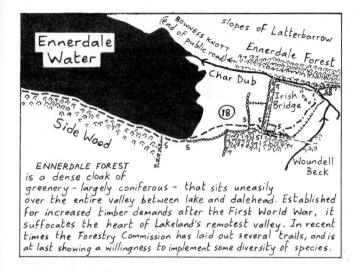

ENNERDALE FOREST is a dense cloak of greenery – largely coniferous – that sits uneasily over the entire valley between lake and dalehead. Established for increased timber demands after the First World War, it suffocates the heart of Lakeland's remotest valley. In recent times the Forestry Commission has laid out several trails, and is at last showing a willingness to implement some diversity of species.

The second half of the lakeside walk runs through the wonderfully natural Side Wood, a section to be savoured in view of the forest stage imminent. From a stile at the end take the right-hand green swath through the bracken in this dead flat strath at the lake-head. At the second wall a forest road is joined, presenting a choice of either going left with it to join the valley road (the simplest option), or following it into the forest, briefly, turning immediately left and within 100 yards left again to leave by another stile. Aim half-right across the field for a footbridge over the Liza, and from the stile in the corner rise up to meet the valley road.

Turn right along the road, which passes Low Gillerthwaite (a field centre) and High Gillerthwaite (a youth hostel) where it loses its surface. The forest road forges on over a cattle-grid deep into the trees, at the same time as a high-level ridgewalk option takes advantage of the break on the left. So, through the forest we go, undeflected by lesser branches or forks. When the great mountains reveal themselves, outstanding is the increasingly powerful outline of Pillar Rock, high up to the right.

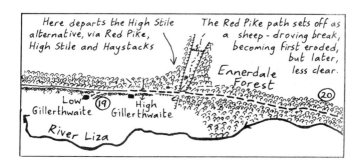

Here departs the High Stile alternative, via Red Pike, High Stile and Haystacks

The Red Pike path sets off as a sheep-droving break, becoming first eroded, but later, less clear.

Ennerdale Forest

Low Gillerthwaite   19   High Gillerthwaite   20

River Liza

Pillar Rock from the forest road. Low cloud on Pillar reveals the majestic tower that gave the mountain its name

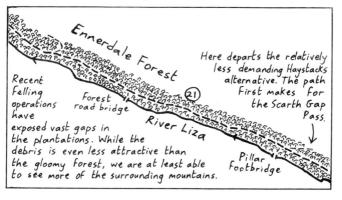

Ennerdale Forest

Recent felling operations have exposed vast gaps in the plantations. While the debris is even less attractive than the gloomy forest, we are at least able to see more of the surrounding mountains.

Forest road bridge   21

River Liza

Here departs the relatively less demanding Haystacks alternative. The path first makes for the Scarth Gap Pass.

Pillar Footbridge

The hard road eventually reaches the end of the forest, and as it swings down to the right, take the gate in front with a glimpse of Black Sail Hut, and even better, Great Gable, beckoning: the path runs broadly on to the youth hostel. After a sojourn in the open spaces of the dalehead, overlooked by Pillar, Kirk Fell and the Gables, do not be swayed by the main path which runs along down to a footbridge over the Liza (a common error), but instead contour along from the hut on a thin path that gradually becomes clearer to arrive at the unmistakable Loft Beck, only yards above its merger with Tongue Beck. On crossing it a well-worn path begins an immediate ascent of its bank, climbing through surroundings so grand that it is as well there is no opportunity to rush through this.

At the top a line of small cairns escort the path up easier ground, with Crummock Water and the slaty Grasmoor Fells appearing across to the left: note also the great near-vertical north wall of Haystacks, closer to hand. The old Ennerdale boundary fence is crossed during its climb to the summit of Brandreth up to the right, while our path motors on its gentler way. Soon the Moses' Trod path will be espied contouring around the flank of Grey Knotts ahead, our path being set on a collision course with it. At the junction go left along the broad way of the Trod, with the hollow of Warnscale Bottom down to the left, and the outspread Buttermere Valley making a memorable scene.

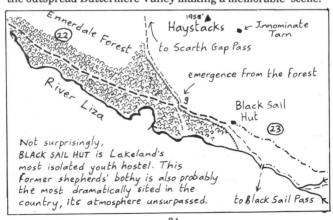

34

Black Sail
Hut,
looking to
Green Gable
and
Great Gable

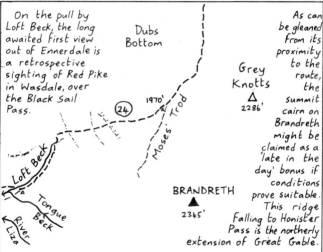

On the pull by Loft Beck, the long awaited first view out of Ennerdale is a retrospective sighting of Red Pike in Wasdale, over the Black Sail Pass.

Dubs Bottom

Grey Knotts
△
2286'

(24) 1970'

Moses' Trod

Loft Beck

Tongue Beck

River Liza

BRANDRETH
▲
2345'

As can be gleaned from its proximity to the route, the summit cairn on Brandreth might be claimed as a 'late in the day' bonus if conditions prove suitable. This ridge falling to Honister Pass is the northerly extension of Great Gable.

MOSES' TROD is a spanking walkers' route through the hills, but did not originate as such. This old way from the quarries above Honister to Wasdale Head (and onward to the coast at Ravenglass) was established for the passage of packhorses laden with slate. Its name recalls one of the great characters of the Honister quarries, whose supposed spare-time occupation of distilling and smuggling whisky gave him further cause to travel this way. ■

The Buttermere Valley from above Moses' Trod

HONISTER PASS - or Hause - is one of Lakeland's better known road passes. Part of its popularity is the ease with which it forms part of a circular tour from Keswick, a facility taken full advantage of well before the advent of the motor car, when trips by waggonette were hampered by the passengers being forced to get out and walk up the steeper sections! The former toll road gives an ideal escape from the traffic, being better graded and affording spectacular views over the mountains encircling the dalehead. Many will consider the descent to Borrowdale to be the most beautiful section of the walk.

While the hinterland of Honister Crag openly displays all the scars of quarrying, its sombre face is itself riddled with tunnels and shafts from the hard days spent prising out the slate - days that have only recently passed into history.

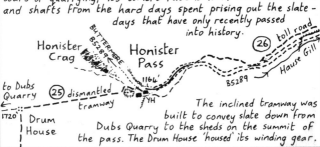

The inclined tramway was built to convey slate down from Dubs Quarry to the sheds on the summit of the pass. The Drum House 'housed' its winding gear.

36

The trod runs down to another major junction at the conspicuous remains of the Drum House. Go right down the course of the dismantled tramway that runs unerringly from the Drum House to the former quarry sheds on the summit of Honister Pass. This is a popular motorists' halt, though the sudden population boom is tempered by the remarkable revelation of Honister Crag falling to the pass on its descent towards Gatesgarth.

Turn right down the road a short way, though at the first opportunity its verges are left in favour of the old Honister road, which rather cleverly keeps generally clear of the motor road as it spirals down to Borrowdale, concluding through the enclosures above Seatoller. Go left through the tiny village, leaving by a stile at the end of the car park. Keeping right at an initial fork, a charming path runs on above the Derwent through Johnny's Wood, terminating at Longthwaite youth hostel. Cross the bridge over the river, and a few yards up the road a path breaks off to the left to run more directly through the fields to Rosthwaite.

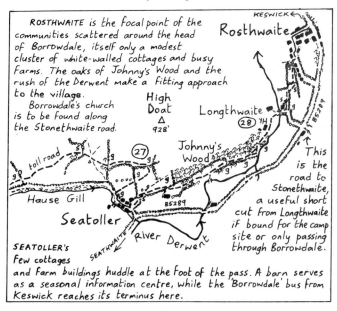

ROSTHWAITE is the focal point of the communities scattered around the head of Borrowdale, itself only a modest cluster of white-walled cottages and busy farms. The oaks of Johnny's Wood and the rush of the Derwent make a fitting approach to the village.

Borrowdale's church is to be found along the Stonethwaite road.

KESWICK

Rosthwaite

High Doat △ 928'

Longthwaite

(28) YH

toll road

(27)

Johnny's Wood

This is the road to Stonethwaite, a useful short cut from Longthwaite if bound for the camp site or only passing through Borrowdale.

Hause Gill

B5289

Seatoller

River Derwent

SEATOLLER's Few cottages and farm buildings huddle at the foot of the pass. A barn serves as a seasonal information centre, while the 'Borrowdale' bus from Keswick reaches its terminus here.

SECTION 3

ROSTHWAITE TO PATTERDALE

17¹/₂ miles

4000 feet of ascent

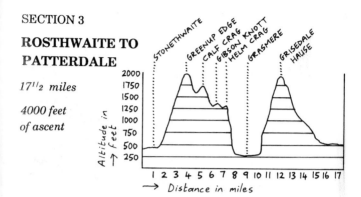

This section walks very much against the grain, faced by a pair of ridges ranged against easterly progress. Clear paths make use of passes in each instance, though as both the Central Ridge and the Helvellyn-Fairfield ridge must be crossed at virtually the 2000ft contour, the prospect of this dual 'ascent' usually encourages an overnight halt at Grasmere. The valley scenery at each end (Stonethwaite and Grisedale) is matched only by the intervening loveliness of the Vale of Grasmere.

If settling for Grasmere, then halving the distance gives opportunity to incorporate high summits into one or both days. Again, with experience and weather on your side, options to Grasmere include a walk from Stonethwaite to Greenup Edge by way of Dock Tarn and Ullscarf, or leaving Greenup Edge for High Raise and Easedale Tarn. A longer Stonethwaite option goes by way of Langstrath, Stake Pass, the Langdale Pikes and Blea Rigg for Easedale. In contrast the direct route from Far Easedale Head down to Grasmere short-cuts the main route.

Beyond Grasmere higher mountains are the only option, being departures from Grisedale Tarn either onto Saint Sunday Crag (not too demanding) or Helvellyn, a stiffer proposition.

If still bent on completing the section in one day, then there is little point in descending all the way to Grasmere's valley level. Instead, drop into Wythburn to meet the A591 above Thirlmere, then up by Dunmail Raise to follow Raise Beck to Grisedale Tarn.

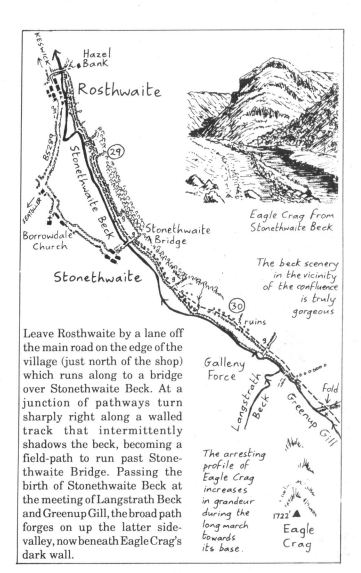

KESWICK

Hazel Bank

Rosthwaite

B5289

Stonethwaite Beck

29

SEATOLLER

Borrowdale Church

Stonethwaite Bridge

Stonethwaite

Eagle Crag from Stonethwaite Beck

The beck scenery in the vicinity of the confluence is truly gorgeous

30

ruins

Galleny Force

Langstrath Beck

Greenup Gill

Fold

The arresting profile of Eagle Crag increases in grandeur during the long march towards its base.

1722' ▲ Eagle Crag

Leave Rosthwaite by a lane off the main road on the edge of the village (just north of the shop) which runs along to a bridge over Stonethwaite Beck. At a junction of pathways turn sharply right along a walled track that intermittently shadows the beck, becoming a field-path to run past Stonethwaite Bridge. Passing the birth of Stonethwaite Beck at the meeting of Langstrath Beck and Greenup Gill, the broad path forges on up the latter side-valley, now beneath Eagle Crag's dark wall.

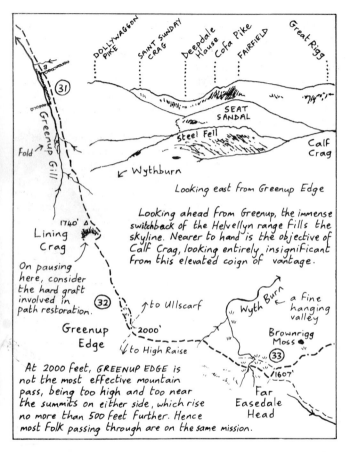

DOLLYWAGGON PIKE · SAINT SUNDAY CRAG · Deepdale Hause · Cofa Pike · FAIRFIELD · Great Rigg

SEAT SANDAL

Steel Fell

Calf Crag

← Wythburn

Looking east from Greenup Edge

Looking ahead from Greenup, the immense switchback of the Helvellyn range fills the skyline. Nearer to hand is the objective of Calf Crag, looking entirely insignificant from this elevated coign of vantage.

Greenup Gill

Fold ↗

1740' △
Lining Crag ↑

On pausing here, consider the hard graft involved in path restoration.

(31)

(32) ↑ to Ullscarf

Greenup Edge

2000'

↓ to High Raise

Wyth Burn · a fine hanging valley

Brownrigg Moss ●

(33)

1607'

Far Easedale Head

At 2000 feet, GREENUP EDGE is not the most effective mountain pass, being too high and too near the summits on either side, which rise no more than 500 feet further. Hence most folk passing through are on the same mission.

Further up the Greenup valley, the path leaves the final wall behind and rises towards the imposing Lining Crag. Through clusters of drumlins the path arrives at the foot of the crag, then climbs adventurously to its left on a restored path. The top of the crag is an amiable green knoll few will pass without a detour, particularly as the next half-hour is much less auspicious: in any case, this is the place to bid farewell to Borrowdale.

Above Lining Crag the gradients relent, and in moist surroundings the cairned path runs on to the summit of the pass on Greenup Edge. The next pass, at Far Easedale Head, is clearly in view several hundred feet below, beyond the head of the intervening valley of Wythburn. The path thereto descends sharply before running across a marshy shelf, a deviation left being little better than the main path, which meets the crest of the pass at a redundant stile.

While the main path heads directly into Far Easedale in the company of the beck, the recommended route takes advantage of height gained to incorporate an extremely easy and hugely rewarding ridgewalk. Along to the left the undulating ridge climbs to Calf Crag, a short half mile distant, then over the crest of Gibson Knott to the prominent Helm Crag out at the end. The short climb to Calf Crag soon reaches its cairned top above a steep fall to Far Easedale, before the path winds along to the twin-cairned top of Gibson Knott. Note that the path does not slavishly adhere to the crest.

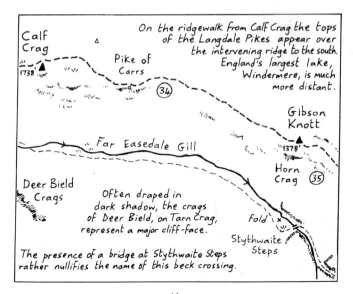

Calf Crag

Pike of Carrs

1738

34

On the ridgewalk from Calf Crag the tops of the Langdale Pikes appear over the intervening ridge to the south. England's largest lake, Windermere, is much more distant.

Gibson Knott

Far Easedale Gill

1378

Horn Crag

35

Deer Bield Crags

Often draped in dark shadow, the crags of Deer Bield, on Tarn Crag, represent a major cliff-face.

Fold

Stythwaite Steps

The presence of a bridge at Stythwaite Steps rather nullifies the name of this beck crossing.

The short descent to the next saddle, Bracken Hause, precedes a final pull to Helm Crag, to be greeted by a knob of rock marking the summit. The path runs along Helm Crag's fascinating crest to similarly appointed outcrops at the other end before commencing a pulsating descent towards the outspread Vale of Grasmere. After a short drop the path runs onto a green knoll, and here turn sharp right on a path that has replaced the erosion-stricken one continuing down the ridge-end. This well-made substitute winds down rather more sedately to meet the valley path in Far Easedale, turning left to quickly become surfaced. This access road heads out through a field and threads a long, pleasant, winding course to Grasmere village.

The summit of HELM CRAG (above) is a bewildering wonderland that deserves careful exploration. The tilted tower of rock pointing skyward is best known as the Howitzer, and demands an adventurous scramble to claim a true ascent of Helm Crag.

Dove Cottage

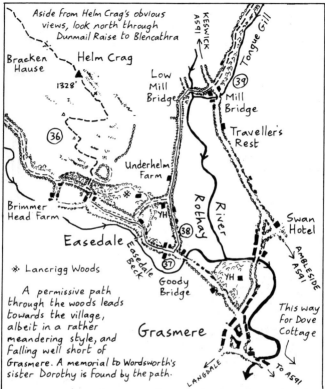

Aside from Helm Crag's obvious views, look north through Dunmail Raise to Blencathra

Bracken Hause

Helm Crag
1328'

36

Low Mill Bridge

KESWICK A591

Tongue Gill

39

Mill Bridge

Traveller's Rest

Underhelm Farm

9

YH

Rothay River

38

Swan Hotel

AMBLESIDE A591

Brimmer Head Farm

Easedale

Easedale Beck

27

Goody Bridge

YH

❋ Lancrigg Woods

A permissive path through the woods leads towards the village, albeit in a rather meandering style, and falling well short of Grasmere. A memorial to Wordsworth's sister Dorothy is found by the path.

Grasmere

This way For Dove Cottage

LANGDALE

TO A591

GRASMERE is famous on two counts, its natural beauty and its literary connections. Gracing its own verdant vale, the physical attributes leave nothing to the imagination. The river Rothay flows into Grasmere's own sheet of water, a quiet mere disturbed only by rowing boats.

Thronged with tourists from around the globe, the village centre is supported by several hamlets along the main road. It is one of these, Town End, that hides Dove Cottage, best known of William Wordsworth's Lakeland homes. The poet rests in the village churchyard, marked by the plainest of headstones. Other attractions at Grasmere include the famous sports, gingerbread, perfumery, Heaton Cooper gallery, and an annual rushbearing.

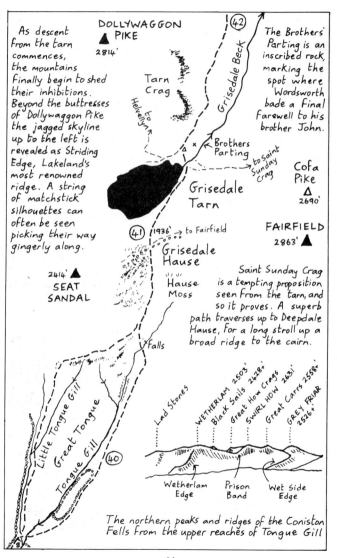

As descent from the tarn commences, the mountains finally begin to shed their inhibitions. Beyond the buttresses of Dollywaggon Pike the jagged skyline up to the left is revealed as Striding Edge, Lakeland's most renowned ridge. A string of matchstick silhouettes can often be seen picking their way gingerly along.

DOLLYWAGGON
▲ PIKE
2814'

Tarn Crag

to Helvellyn

42

Grisedale Beck

The Brothers' Parting is an inscribed rock, marking the spot where Wordsworth bade a final farewell to his brother John.

△ ×← Brothers Parting

Grisedale Tarn

to Saint Sunday Crag

Cofa Pike
△
2690'

FAIRFIELD
2863' ▲

41 1936' → to Fairfield

Grisedale Hause

2414' ▲
SEAT SANDAL

Hause Moss

Saint Sunday Crag is a tempting proposition seen from the tarn, and so it proves. A superb path traverses up to Deepdale Hause, for a long stroll up a broad ridge to the cairn.

Falls

Little Tongue Gill

Great Tongue

Tongue Gill

40

Lad Stones

WETHERLAM 2503'
Black Sails 2428'
Great How Crags
SWIRL HOW 2631'
Great Carrs 2558'
GREY FRIAR 2526'+

Wetherlam Edge   Prison Band   Wet Side Edge

The northern peaks and ridges of the Coniston Fells from the upper reaches of Tongue Gill

44

Departure from Grasmere (see previous map) is along the side-road leaving Easedale Road at Goody Bridge for Thorney How youth hostel, continuing on to a junction and then up to the A591 at Mill Bridge. Cross straight over the busy road and up a time-honoured track faithfully signposted to Patterdale.

When it gains the open fell a choice awaits, for well-worn paths run either side of Great Tongue, directly in front, to rejoin much higher up. The left-hand one is the old pony track, the other a less historic walkers' alternative. They meet under the abrupt eastern bluff of Seat Sandal, in readiness for gaining the top of Grisedale Hause. This is a fine moment, with Grisedale Tarn immediately below and the unremitting wall of Dollywaggon Pike dispelling many a notion of a detour over Helvellyn. Eminently more inviting is the noble profile of Saint Sunday Crag beyond the tarn's outflow, and if considering an alternative route to Patterdale, then this presents the easier option.

For the moment, however, descend to the foot of the tarn, one of the most popular picnic spots in the district. Certainly the mountain atmosphere here is strong, even if none show their finest faces. On leaving, the main route crosses the outflow to begin the descent to Patterdale by way of Grisedale's long but easy miles.

The head of Ullswater from Saint Sunday Crag's north-east ridge

After passing the 'Brothers' Parting' stone, the path descends to Ruthwaite Lodge, a little below which is a fork. Either route will be enjoyed, the traditional one dropping down to the right to a footbridge over the beck and continuing without ado to the valley floor. The left branch crosses Ruthwaite Beck and remains on the north side of the valley, on the lower flanks of Striding Edge. It meets the Striding Edge path at its foot to join the main route (by now a farm road) in the valley bottom. This narrow road drops down to the main road north of the village, though part-way down a gate on the right shows the way to a stile just above, from where an attractive finish through the trees of Glemara Park draws the day to a more suitable conclusion.

Entry into Patterdale is by way of Mill Moss and the public conveniences.

GRISEDALE is a long, uncomplicated valley, reminiscent of a Highland glen. From the bridge at its foot, the peaks through which the pass has brought us are now seen at their rugged best. Only a farm road penetrates the dale floor.

Nethermostcove Beck

Spout Crag

Ruthwaite Beck

Ruthwaite Lodge

Grisedale Beck

(43)

(44)

barn

Elmhow

Grisedale Beck

Saint Sunday Crag from Grisedale Beck

Ruthwaite Lodge was a climbers' hut until a fire destroyed it.

46

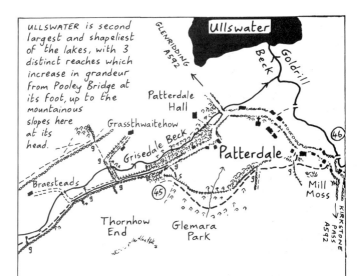

ULLSWATER is second largest and shapeliest of the lakes, with 3 distinct reaches which increase in grandeur from Pooley Bridge at its foot, up to the mountainous slopes here at its head.

Ullswater

Glenridding A592

Goldrill Beck

Patterdale Hall

Grassthwaitehow

Grisedale Beck

Patterdale

(46)

Braesteads

(45)

Mill Moss

Kirkstone Pass A592

Thornhow End

Glemara Park

PATTERDALE is the undisputed capital of the Ullswater valley, standing at the head of the lake in the broad, green strath of the Goldrill Beck. It is not a large settlement, its various components being strung out along the A592. 'St. Patrick's Dale' is an extremely popular resort, but its lack of size has helped preserve it from the excessive commercialism of other central Lakeland villages. Boating and pony trekking are much enjoyed peaceful pastimes, while the slopes of the north-eastern Helvellyn range appeal to the ski-ing fraternity.

Although Patterdale is hemmed in by mountains, a motor road escapes north clinging to Ullswater's shore, and also south over the Kirkstone Pass. This connects with Windermere and Ambleside, and at the 1479 ft. summit it squeezes between fells a further thousand feet higher. On the very top is the former 'Travellers' Rest', which is the second highest inn in the country.

Goldrill House, Patterdale YH

SECTION 4

PATTERDALE
TO SHAP

16 miles

*2700 feet
of ascent*

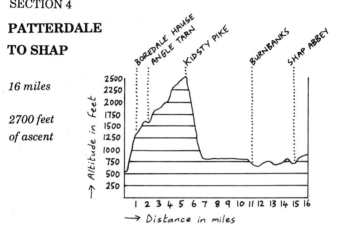

The enormous High Street ridge stands between us and faster progress towards the Yorkshire coast, and a promising forecast is especially appreciated for the morning of departure. While High Street is the parent fell of the group, an entire family of interlinking ridges spew forth from the windswept skyline that is the summit of the Coast to Coast Walk. The pass of Boredale Hause and the intricate curves of Angle Tarn break up the climb to the Straits of Riggindale, where a clear day gives views far to the east, to Pennine country. From Kidsty Pike's precipitous crest the shore of Haweswater is soon alongside, and remains so until the final miles run through the verdant country of the river Lowther to Shap Abbey, well hidden from its village.

The nature of intervening valleys drilling deep into the hills makes this the only logical route, save for the enthusiast using it as a springboard to claim higher summits on and about the ridge. However, if an alternative is sought, usually due to poor weather, then a lower level, slightly longer walk follows Ullswater's shore to Howtown, there taking a bridleway onto Moor Divock to descend to the Lowther valley north of Bampton. This is not a poor alternative, but actually a very enjoyable and relatively easy one.

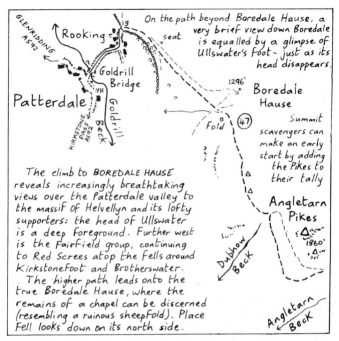

On the path beyond Boredale Hause, a very brief view down Boredale is equalled by a glimpse of Ullswater's Foot - just as its head disappears.

GLENRIDDING A592

Rooking

seat

Goldrill Bridge

Patterdale

YH

KIRKSTONE PASS A592

Goldrill Beck

1296'

Fold

47

Boredale Hause

Summit scavengers can make an early start by adding the Pikes to their tally

Angletarn Pikes

1860'

Dubhow Beck

Angletarn Beck

The climb to BOREDALE HAUSE reveals increasingly breathtaking views over the Patterdale valley to the massif of Helvellyn and its lofty supporters: the head of Ullswater is a deep foreground. Further west is the Fairfield group, continuing to Red Screes atop the fells around Kirkstonefoot and Brotherswater.

The higher path leads onto the true Boredale Hause, where the remains of a chapel can be discerned (resembling a ruinous sheepfold). Place Fell looks down on its north side.

Leave the village by the side-road branching off just south of the *White Lion,* swinging round to the left to terminate in a corner. A gate on the right gains the open fell, and a path slants away up to the right. At a fork below a seat keep to the lower path to rise effortlessly and quickly onto the broad, grassy saddle of Boredale Hause.

When the going eases at a pair of cairns on a green plinth, cross the tiny beck above a sheepfold to a path winding up to the right. Tamer surrounds crowds in briefly before emergence above the head of Dubhow Beck, a classic moment as Brotherswater appears dramatically far below. A choice of higher or lower paths traverse the flank of Angletarn Pikes to the same goal, rounding a corner to find Angle Tarn outspread in front, and the great line of the High Street range marching across the skyline high above.

Looking back from Angle Tarn to the previous stage

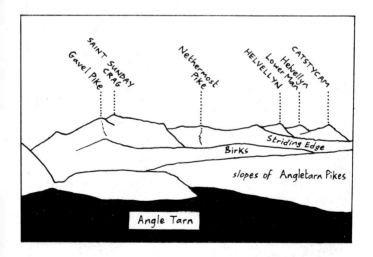

Gavel Pike
SAINT SUNDAY CRAG
Nethermost Pike
HELVELLYN
Lower Man
Helvellyn
CATSTYCAM

Striding Edge

Birks

slopes of Angletarn Pikes

Angle Tarn

The path rounds the far side of the tarn and continues up to a gate below Satura Crag, before heading on through peaty terrain below Rest Dodd. The whole of Hayeswater appears ahead beneath Thornthwaite Crag, and an undulating trek ensues before climbing to the dome of The Knott, merging with a path from Hartsop to reach a wall-corner just beneath the summit.

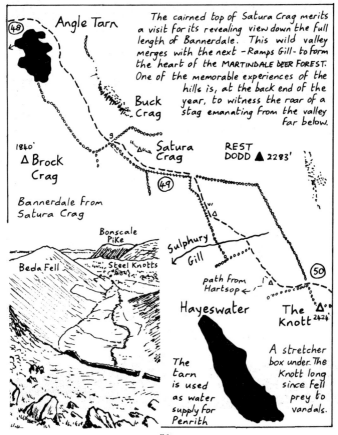

Angle Tarn

(48)

The cairned top of Satura Crag merits a visit for its revealing view down the full length of Bannerdale. This wild valley merges with the next – Ramps Gill – to form the heart of the MARTINDALE DEER FOREST. One of the memorable experiences of the hills is, at the back end of the year, to witness the roar of a stag emanating from the valley far below.

Buck Crag

1840'
Δ Brock Crag

Satura Crag

REST DODD ▲ 2283'

(49)

Bannerdale from Satura Crag

Bonscale Pike

Beda Fell   Steel Knotts

Sulphury Gill

path from Hartsop ←

(50)

Hayeswater

The Knott 2424'

The tarn is used as water supply for Penrith

A stretcher box under The Knott long since fell prey to vandals.

Kidsty Pike from Twopenny Crag

The great whaleback of High Street is just ahead now, and the path runs along the wallside to the airy saddle of the Straits of Riggindale. Double back sharply from this path junction to skirt round the rim of Riggindale to the waiting peak of Kidsty Pike, very much a place for an extended break. Far below at the foot of Riggindale, Haweswater shimmers, and when it's time to leave a clear path quickly forms to pass a brace of shelters on a rash of stones on the declining east ridge.

The HIGH STREET ROMAN ROAD is a legendary old highway linking the fort at Brougham, near Penrith, with Ambleside. It was their highest way in the country, reaching almost 2700 feet on the fell that now bears its name. The bare, exposed mountain top saw further action a couple of centuries ago, as the venue of horse races and sports linked with the Mardale shepherds' meet.

KIDSTY PIKE has an impressive profile which masks the fact it is merely a minor upthrust on the shoulder of another mountain. Its spectacular drop into Riggindale is no sham, however, nor its position for appraising the craggy eastern face of High Street - or hoping to glimpse a shy deer or a rather special bird.

Ramps Gill

▲ HIGH RAISE 2631'

High Street Roman road

Rampsgill Head 2598' △

51 Kidsty Pike 2558' △

Randale Beck

Twopenny Crag

Sale Pot ← a textbook example of a hanging valley

Straits of Riggindale

High Street Roman road

Short Stile

↓ summit of High Street

Riggindale Beck

The path descends all the way to the lakeshore, taking the knobbly crest of Kidsty Howes in its stride. At the foot of the ridge join the lakeside path, turning left over a bridge over Randale Beck and then along the entire length of Haweswater on a clear path throughout, always with a wall or fence keeping us from polluting the water.

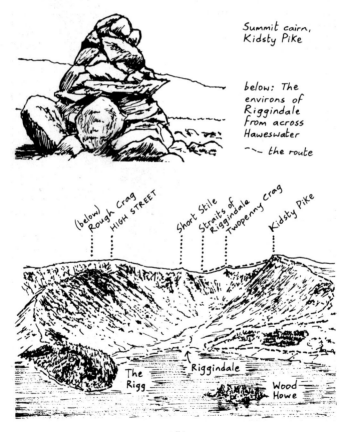

Summit cairn, Kidsty Pike

below: The environs of Riggindale from across Haweswater

--- the route

(below) Rough Crag
HIGH STREET
Short Stile
Straits of Riggindale
Twopenny Crag
Kidsty Pike

The Rigg

Riggindale

Wood Howe

Old maps and faded photographs only serve to intensify the crying shame of a valley that was stolen. Until the flooding of MARDALE in the 1930s, a tiny village with its near-legendary 'Dun Bull' inn and a range of farmsteads shared the dale with Haweswater, but all the habitations were drowned or left to collapse with the construction of a massive dam. Few can remember the old place, and the kick in the teeth is the fact that in times of drought it becomes a tourist attraction – they even plunder the old stones as souvenirs.

Whelter Knotts ⑤④

Whelter Beck

Whelter Crags

Randale Beck

⑤②

Kidsty Howes

hillfort
1300'
Castle Crag

⑤③

Rigging Beck

The Rigg

Speaking Crag

Wood Howe

Haweswater

Best appraised during descent to the lakeshore, the confined crest of CASTLE CRAG was clearly a logical site for a hillfort. Probably dating from the Iron age, evidence of hearths and hut floors has been uncovered.

The presence of England's only nesting Golden Eagles on the crags above Riggindale is a major visitor draw, with a public observation hut (R.S.P.B.) just off-route near the foot of Riggindale Beck.

⑤⑤

Haweswater and Harter Fell from the path near Measand Beck

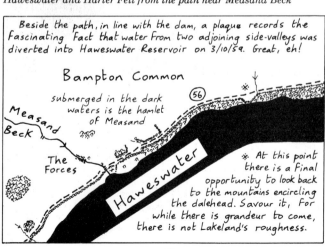

Beside the path, in line with the dam, a plaque records the fascinating fact that water from two adjoining side-valleys was diverted into Haweswater Reservoir on 3/10/59. Great, eh!

Bampton Common

submerged in the dark waters is the hamlet of Measand

56

Measand Beck

The Forces

Haweswater

* At this point there is a final opportunity to look back to the mountains encircling the dalehead. Savour it, for while there is grandeur to come, there is not Lakeland's roughness.

In its later stages the way becomes a broad track to drop to a stile by a gate, then descends through trees to a rough road down to the cottages at Burnbanks. Go left along the road out of the hamlet, but within a minute locate a gateway on the right, from where a path runs through delightful woodland to where Naddle Bridge strides over Haweswater Beck. Cross the road to descend to more woodland, but at once also cross the main beck by a parallel defunct old pack-bridge, and inflowing Naddle Beck by a footbridge - an interesting corner!

Head downstream in the lovely environs of the beck, passing Thornthwaite Force and shapely Park Bridge in quick succession. After a brief break from the beck, a wide track forms to soon rise above a wooded bank to cross a side-stream to a stile. Here forsake the valley of Haweswater Beck by following the fence-side up to the barns of High Park, then steer left up the field towards a stile in a fence.

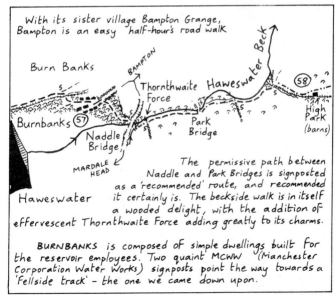

With its sister village Bampton Grange, Bampton is an easy half-hour's road walk

Burn Banks

BAMPTON

Thornthwaite Force

Haweswater Beck

58

Burnbanks 57

Naddle Bridge

MARDALE HEAD

Park Bridge

High Park (barns)

Haweswater

The permissive path between Naddle and Park Bridges is signposted as a 'recommended' route, and recommended it certainly is. The beckside walk is in itself a wooded delight, with the addition of effervescent Thornthwaite Force adding greatly to its charms.

BURNBANKS is composed of simple dwellings built for the reservoir employees. Two quaint MCWW (Manchester Corporation Water Works) signposts point the way towards a 'fellside track' - the one we came down upon.

SHAP ABBEY is the only abbey in old Westmorland, and is a rarity also in its proximity to the high mountains. Founded around the end of the 12th century, it housed White Canons belonging to the Premonstratensian order (see also Easby, near Richmond). The tower presides over otherwise low-lying ruins, much of the stone having found its way into the adjoining Farm. Its setting, as ever, is idyllic, and the cost to savour it? Nothing at all.

The RIVER LOWTHER flows for sixteen miles from the dam of Wet Sleddale Reservoir to its entry into the Eamont near Penrith. Its grassy banks are emphatically free of man's interference, the only settlement to take advantage being Bampton Grange, which can hardly be regarded as a blemish.

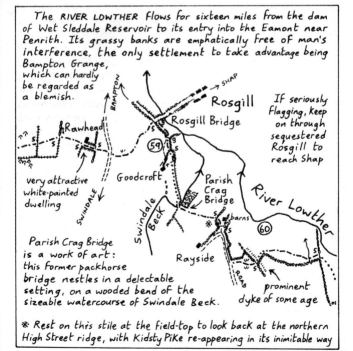

If seriously Flagging, keep on through sequestered Rosgill to reach Shap

very attractive white-painted dwelling

Parish Crag Bridge is a work of art: this former packhorse bridge nestles in a delectable setting, on a wooded bend of the sizeable watercourse of Swindale Beck.

prominent dyke of some age

✱ Rest on this stile at the field-top to look back at the northern High Street ridge, with Kidsty Pike re-appearing in its inimitable way

The sketchy path runs a direct course through a couple more fields to Rawhead Farm, following its drive out onto an open road. Cross straight over on a path that bears left over open country to descend to another road at Rosgill Bridge. Barely impinging on the tarmac, however, turn immediately right onto a farm drive heading downstream by the river Lowther. At the next gate forsake the drive and keep left with a wall, passing below the farm of Good Croft and along a fence-side to discover Parish Crag Bridge crossing Swindale Beck. Up the bank behind bear left up the field towards a barn on the skyline, passing through an enclosure occupied by a motley assortment of barns to meet a narrow road on a corner.

Turn up the road until the accompanying wall breaks off to the left, then do likewise by aiming across to a stile beyond marshy ground. Follow the wall away to a corner, from where a thin path runs through a large field, short-cutting the wide curve of the wall up to the right. On the brow the tower of Shap Abbey appears, and from a stile at the far corner, a final field is crossed to meet the Lowther again just before the abbey. Abbey Bridge leads into the abbey car park and onto the road climbing away, but the abbey ruins can first be inspected by means of the green track on the right. Back at Abbey Bridge, the concrete road climbs steeply (cruelly so, at this stage) through a field, becoming a narrow lane to meet another road running along to enter Shap.

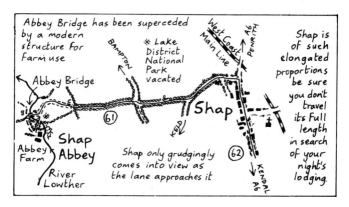

Abbey Bridge has been superceded by a modern structure for farm use

West Coast Main Line

A6 PENRITH

BAMPTON

* Lake District National Park vacated

Abbey Bridge

Shap

61

KELD

Shap is of such elongated proportions be sure you don't travel its full length in search of your night's lodging.

Shap Abbey

Abbey Farm

River Lowther

Shap only grudgingly comes into view as the lane approaches it

62

KENDAL A6

SHAP TO KIRKBY STEPHEN

20 miles   *1600 feet of ascent*

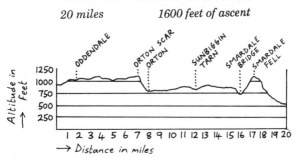

A marvellous range of scenery is matched by a remarkable concentration of features deeply rooted in history during this long but easy walk. This crossing of the Westmorland plateau is dominated by limestone underfoot and distant views of rolling hills: back to Lakeland, south to the Howgill Fells, and east to the Pennines. The only village encountered is Orton, a pleasant interlude between the stone circles, prehistoric settlements and burial chambers, and a large tarn that form integral parts of this grand march.

There is little scope for finding a shorter way, but certainly alternatives exist, either southerly on the Roman road to Orton and then through the upper Lune valley to Newbiggin on Lune and perhaps Ravenstonedale; or northerly to Crosby Ravensworth, Bank Moor, Little Asby, Potts Valley and Crosby Garrett.

Please be aware that route changes are likely at Crosby Ravensworth Fell, Sunbiggin Tarn and Severals.

Market Hall, Shap

Shap is hardly jigsaw material, but it can boast this fine building. 300 years old, it stands midway along the main street (west side).

Leave the main street by suburban Moss Grove opposite the *Kings Arms,* soon turning right on a road that becomes a rough track climbing to a bridge over the railway line. Continuing between hedgerows, bear right at a fork beyond a barn, our green way soon emerging into a field. With the outline of a motorway footbridge ahead, three fields are crossed to earn the satisfaction of crossing the M6, a landmark event.

What is more important however is the fact that Kirkby Stephen is 20 miles distant, so press on by turning right on the other side. Beyond a wall-end the thin path slants up through boulders and hawthorn to a brow, below which is the Hardendale road alongside the isolated house of The Nab. Cross over and bear right on a thin green way to a wall-corner, rising slightly to approach Hardendale Quarry. Beyond a fence a stile on the right leads to a pair of step-flights decorating the quarry road.

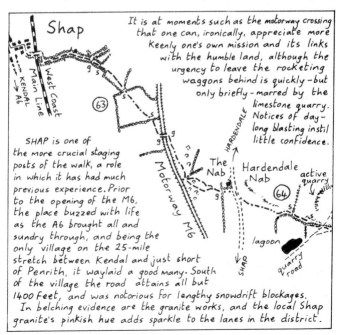

Shap

It is at moments such as the motorway crossing that one can, ironically, appreciate more keenly one's own mission and its links with the humble land, although the urgency to leave the rocketing waggons behind is quickly – but only briefly – marred by the limestone quarry. Notices of day-long blasting instil little confidence.

SHAP is one of the more crucial staging posts of the walk, a role in which it has had much previous experience. Prior to the opening of the M6, the place buzzed with life as the A6 brought all and sundry through, and being the only village on the 25-mile stretch between Kendal and just short of Penrith, it waylaid a good many. South of the village the road attains all but 1400 feet, and was notorious for lengthy snowdrift blockages.

In belching evidence are the granite works, and the local Shap granite's pinkish hue adds sparkle to the lanes in the district.

On the other side a dusty road heads away to Oddendale, hidden in trees, but at the entrance keep outside its confines on a similarly broad track rising onto the grassy moor. Easily missed is Oddendale Stone Circle across to the right, as the broad green track runs on to a large, walled enclosure. Keeping left of it a slight green way strides on, with Crosby Ravensworth Fell outspread ahead. Continuing on to a slight depression, bear down to the left past a crumbling bield to the corner of a plantation, from where a slim path heads up the easy slope beyond. The distinct course of a Roman road is crossed to rise to a tumulus marked by a signpost - a useful guide.

Head on through a modest limestone pavement to drop to an immense Shap granite boulder. The clear path now descends to cross the embryo Lyvennet and rises to a wall-corner, with the Black Dub monument a little upstream.

The Monument at Black Dub
- inscribed thus -

HERE AT BLACK DUB
THE SOURCE OF THE LIVENNET
KING CHARLES THE II
REGALED HIS ARMY
AND DRANK OF THE WATER
ON HIS MARCH FROM SCOTLAND
AUGUST 8 1651

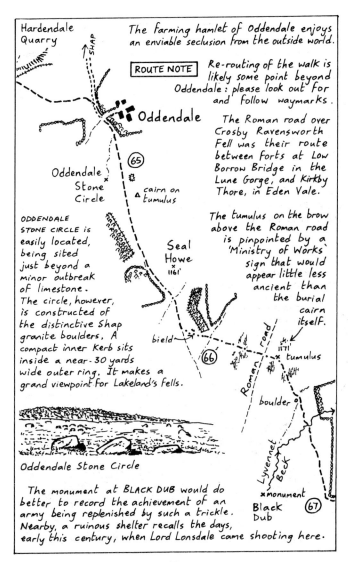

Hardendale
Quarry

The farming hamlet of Oddendale enjoys an enviable seclusion from the outside world.

SHAP

ROUTE NOTE Re-routing of the walk is likely some point beyond Oddendale : please look out for and follow waymarks.

Oddendale

(65)

Oddendale
Stone
Circle

cairn on
△ tumulus

The Roman road over Crosby Ravensworth Fell was their route between forts at Low Borrow Bridge in the Lune Gorge, and Kirkby Thore, in Eden Vale.

ODDENDALE STONE CIRCLE is easily located, being sited just beyond a minor outbreak of limestone. The circle, however, is constructed of the distinctive Shap granite boulders. A compact inner kerb sits inside a near-30 yards wide outer ring. It makes a grand viewpoint for Lakeland's fells.

Seal
Howe
× 1161'

The tumulus on the brow above the Roman road is pinpointed by a 'Ministry of Works' sign that would appear little less ancient than the burial cairn itself.

bield

(66)

Roman road

1171'
× tumulus

boulder

Oddendale Stone Circle

The monument at BLACK DUB would do better to record the achievement of an army being replenished by such a trickle. Nearby, a ruinous shelter recalls the days, early this century, when Lord Lonsdale came shooting here.

Lyvennet Beck

× monument

Black
Dub

(67)

63

At the corner the wall is followed away, descending around the outside of park-like country, past Robin Hood's Grave and then climbing away. When the wall parts company, head over the brow, and with an old quarry as a target, descend to a makeshift stile in a fence lining the moorland road from Orton to Crosby Ravensworth. Slanting right, cross over to a slender trod heading into the obvious recess of a dry valley below an alien plantation. The thin path is followed up to its demise at the meeting of the previous road with the B6260 to Appleby, a superb moment with the Howgill Fells gloriously revealed beyond the patchwork pastures of the upper Lune Valley.

Crossing the cattle-grid the main route, since the demise of Wainwright's crossing of the limestone uplands, heads straight down the road into Orton. While certainly the quickest way, it is, unfortunately, dogged by rather a lot of traffic linking the Appleby area with the motorway at Tebay. The road forges straight into the village centre.

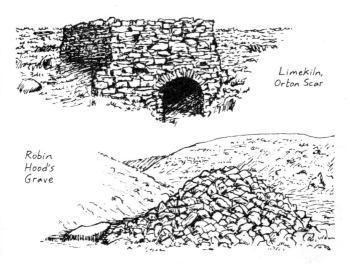

Limekiln,
Orton Scar

Robin
Hood's
Grave

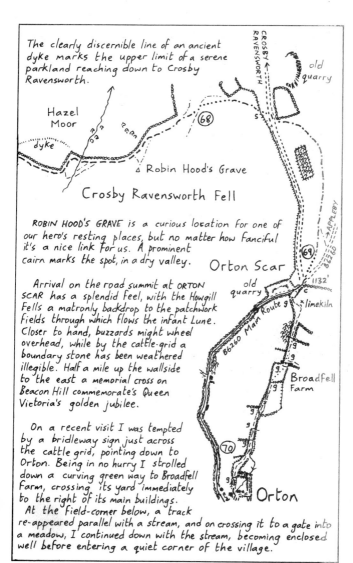

The clearly discernible line of an ancient dyke marks the upper limit of a serene parkland reaching down to Crosby Ravensworth.

CROSBY RAVENSWORTH

old quarry

Hazel Moor

dyke

68

△ Robin Hood's Grave

Crosby Ravensworth Fell

ROBIN HOOD'S GRAVE is a curious location for one of our hero's resting places, but no matter how fanciful it's a nice link for us. A prominent cairn marks the spot, in a dry valley.

B6260 APPLEBY

69

Orton Scar

Arrival on the road summit at ORTON SCAR has a splendid feel, with the Howgill Fells a matronly backdrop to the patchwork fields through which flows the infant Lune. Closer to hand, buzzards might wheel overhead, while by the cattle-grid a boundary stone has been weathered illegible. Half a mile up the wallside to the east a memorial cross on Beacon Hill commemorate's Queen Victoria's golden jubilee.

old quarry

1132'

limekiln

B6260 Main Route

Broadfell Farm

On a recent visit I was tempted by a bridleway sign just across the cattle grid, pointing down to Orton. Being in no hurry I strolled down a curving green way to Broadfell Farm, crossing its yard immediately to the right of its main buildings.

70

Orton

At the field-corner below, a track re-appeared parallel with a stream, and on crossing it to a gate into a meadow, I continued down with the stream, becoming enclosed well before entering a quiet corner of the village.

At Orton

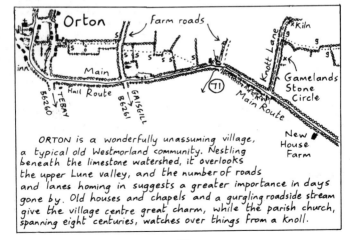

ORTON is a wonderfully unassuming village, a typical old Westmorland community. Nestling beneath the limestone watershed, it overlooks the upper Lune valley, and the number of roads and lanes homing in suggests a greater importance in days gone by. Old houses and chapels and a gurgling roadside stream give the village centre great charm, while the parish church, spanning eight centuries, watches over things from a knoll.

The main route departs the village by continuing through on the road past the inn, bearing left at the edge of the village and out along the road to Raisbeck. At the point where the unsurfaced Knott Lane heads up to the left, there is an opportunity, part way up it, to look over the wall on the right and view Gamelands Stone Circle. The road, meanwhile, runs quickly on to enter Raisbeck.

At Raisbeck, the main route remains on the road still further, eventually emerging from enclosure at a cattle-grid onto the open moor before reaching Sunbiggin Tarn. An attractive option at Raisbeck is to turn left on the cul-de-sac lane to the farming hamlet of Sunbiggin, keeping on the road to its demise, where a green lane takes up the running.

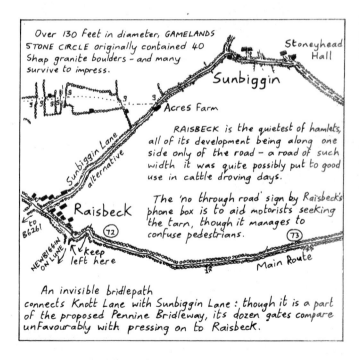

Over 130 feet in diameter, GAMELANDS STONE CIRCLE originally contained 40 Shap granite boulders - and many survive to impress.

Stoneyhead Hall

Sunbiggin

Acres Farm

RAISBECK is the quietest of hamlets, all of its development being along one side only of the road - a road of such width it was quite possibly put to good use in cattle droving days.

The 'no through road' sign by Raisbeck's phone box is to aid motorists seeking the tarn, though it manages to confuse pedestrians.

Sunbiggin Lane alternative

Raisbeck

to B6261

72

73

NEWBIGGIN ON LUNE

keep left here

Main Route

An invisible bridlepath connects Knott Lane with Sunbiggin Lane: though it is a part of the proposed Pennine Bridleway, its dozen gates compare unfavourably with pressing on to Raisbeck.

Above: Sunbiggin Tarn

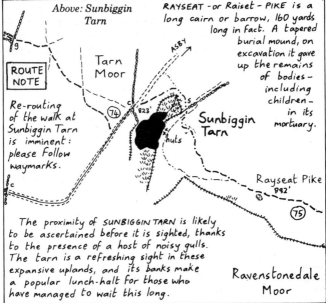

RAYSEAT - or Raiset - PIKE is a long cairn or barrow, 160 yards long in fact. A tapered burial mound, on excavation it gave up the remains of bodies – including children – in its mortuary.

Tarn Moor

ASBY

ROUTE NOTE

74 823'

Sunbiggin Tarn

huts

Re-routing of the walk at Sunbiggin Tarn is imminent: please follow waymarks.

Rayseat Pike 892'

75

The proximity of SUNBIGGIN TARN is likely to be ascertained before it is sighted, thanks to the presence of a host of noisy gulls. The tarn is a refreshing sight in these expansive uplands, and its banks make a popular lunch-halt for those who have managed to wait this long.

Ravenstonedale Moor

The pleasant lane emerges onto heathery Tarn Moor. Heading away to a crossroads in a hollow, turn right then bear almost immediately left at a fork to arrive on a brow with a good prospect of Sunbiggin Tarn below: the track runs unerringly down to the road alongside it. Cross the cattle-grid and slant down to the right, skirting round the marshy head of the tarn to a ladder-stile where a fence and wall meet. A path slants up to a broad track, which runs along to the right to a pair of huts on the shore, a popular lunch halt. This however is a source of confusion, for the route 'proper' bears up to the left before the huts, through a green patch in the heather to a few limestone outcrops and shakeholes.

Rising gradually but sketchily, a thin but very distinct path forges on through the heather, and on the brow the distinctive barrow of Rayseat Pike is seen ahead across a depression. The path is immediately broader now, and in the depression it picks up a path formed by walkers continuing on the natural line past the huts. All is now plain sailing, the path rising past the limestone rocks on the ancient mound and then snaking off through the heather. It deposits us on a moor road at a cattle-grid, and once across head away with the wall skirting Ewefell Mire to a gate at the far end. The track continues away under Great Ewe Fell, passing an advertisement for Bents Farm, which is rather handy if you can't go a step further.

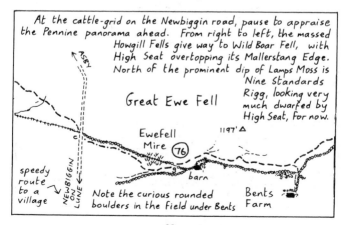

At the cattle-grid on the Newbiggin road, pause to appraise the Pennine panorama ahead. From right to left, the massed Howgill Fells give way to Wild Boar Fell, with High Seat overtopping its Mallerstang Edge. North of the prominent dip of Lamps Moss is Nine Standards Rigg, looking very much dwarfed by High Seat, for now.

Great Ewe Fell

Ewefell Mire (76)

1197' △

speedy route to a village

NEWBIGGIN ON LUNE

barn

Note the curious rounded boulders in the field under Bents

Bents Farm

A685

The expanses of Crosby Garrett Fell are an archaeologists' paradise, and the largest of its prehistoric field systems is

Crosby Garrett Fell

the SEVERALS village settlement. Best appraised in aerial pictures is this labyrinth of grassy mounds that formed hut enclosures at the 'centre' of converging field boundaries. The path has been re-routed to halt its march through the middle.

As well as the impressive viaduct, look for the 'on-site' quarry in this fascinating side-valley of SMARDALE

An important nature reserve now exists here

Smardalegill Viaduct (Former Tebay-Darlington line)

earthwork on brow

railway cottages

IMPORTANT
Further re-routing is planned to help preserve Severals from a trampling: please be sure to follow any waymarks.

Severals

Giants' Graves

good views down Smardale

Smardale Bridge

Public paths at either end of Smardale Bridge lead through a 16th century deer park to Ravenstonedale, a lovely village no matter how tired one might be.

The intriguingly named GIANTS' GRAVES are shown more descriptively on maps as 'pillow mounds' and are of uncertain origin. A possibility is that they were constructed as rabbit warrens, almost at any time since their introduction into Britain by the Normans.

Smardale Bridge

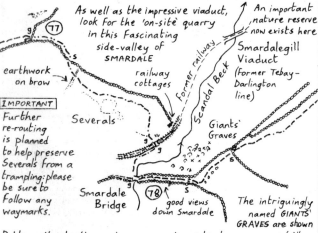

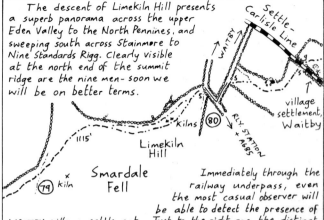

The descent of Limekiln Hill presents a superb panorama across the upper Eden Valley to the North Pennines, and sweeping south across Stainmore to Nine Standards Rigg. Clearly visible at the north end of the summit ridge are the nine men- soon we will be on better terms.

Settle-Carlisle Line

WAITBY

Settle-Carlisle Line

village settlement, Waitby

Kilns (80)

RLY STATION + ALSO

1115

Limekiln Hill

Smardale Fell

(79) kiln

Immediately through the railway underpass, even the most casual observer will be able to detect the presence of WAITBY village settlement. Just to the right are the distinct outlines of a rectangular earthwork with an arrangement of internal enclosures, not all destroyed by the railway embankment.

The SETTLE-CARLISLE RAILWAY is probably the most famous line in the country, thanks largely to the monumental campaign that culminated in its salvation in 1989. As we encounter it, it has just broken free of the enveloping Pennines, and is set for a triumphant journey through the Eden Valley.

The green track continues along the wallside beyond Bents as far as the next gate in the wall. From it follow a wall away to a stile, then slant up to the brow to be greeted by a fine prospect of Smardale, with the route climbing the opposite slope. For now though, a thin path descends pleasantly by Severals village settlement, curving down to a bridge over a former railway line. Go right a short way to descend to the waiting Smardale Bridge.

Across it a superb old road breasts the steep slope, which soon relents to enjoy a gentle traverse of the wide open spaces of Smardale Fell. All too soon it descends above two limekilns to a stile onto a back lane. Follow it right on its central green strip just as far as a junction, then go left to another stile on the right. A thin way winds round a large field to a railway underpass ahead, from which bear gently right to locate a stile by a wall-corner.

The Parish Church, Kirkby Stephen

Just into the field is the long-awaited first glimpse of Kirkby Stephen - a long day is drawing to a close! Stakes guide the way down through a large pasture to a stile at the bottom, then descending past an island barn to a defunct double underpass to enter the yard of Green Riggs Farm.

The way is clearly marked through two gates on the right and then out along the farm road all the way to Kirkby, passing the flat-topped site of Croglam Castle just up to the right. The back lane - not a classic entry to the town - can be followed as far as is desired in order to avoid the main road, though it can be joined much earlier. A fitting way is to keep on as far as the rear of the *Pennine Hotel,* just past which an alleyway leads into the town centre exactly opposite the Market Place - the point at which it will be left.

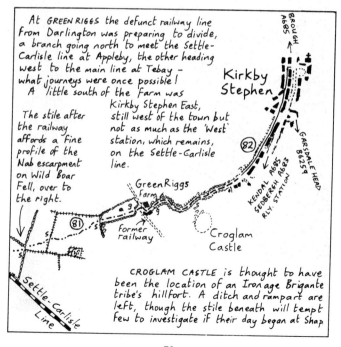

At GREEN RIGGS the defunct railway line from Darlington was preparing to divide, a branch going north to meet the Settle-Carlisle line at Appleby, the other heading west to the main line at Tebay — what journeys were once possible!

A little south of the farm was Kirkby Stephen East, still west of the town but not as much as the 'West' station, which remains, on the Settle-Carlisle line.

The stile after the railway affords a fine profile of the Nab escarpment on Wild Boar Fell, over to the right.

CROGLAM CASTLE is thought to have been the location of an Iron age Brigante tribe's hillfort. A ditch and rampart are left, though the stile beneath will tempt few to investigate if their day began at Shap

SECTION 6

KIRKBY STEPHEN
TO KELD

13 miles

1900 feet of ascent

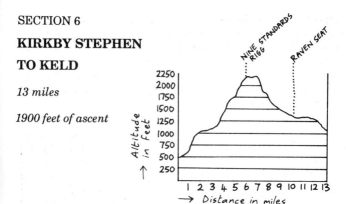

This is the crossing of the Pennine watershed, the backbone of England. Nine Standards Rigg is also a very suitable place to celebrate such an occasion, being an outstanding viewpoint and endowed with various adornments of which the famous Nine Standards are pre-eminent. The ascent is remarkably easy, for the most part on grass verges or green trackways: only the upper limits remind you that a mountain has been climbed. The long descent to the headwaters of the Swale is true Pennine in character, a wild country that is changed little by the arrival of Whitsundale's side-valley, and only on nearing Keld is there a warmer feel.

Bad weather need not bar progress here, for running roughly parallel throughout the whole day is the B6270 road from Nateby to Swaledale, and being largely unenclosed and generally quiet its verges are less of a trial than might be imagined. In any case, the bridleway from the road-end above Fell House could be used in any conditions, and the higher ground omitted by remaining with the wall enclosing Dukerdale to cross south to meet the road at its summit on Lamps Moss. Similarly, lower down Birkdale, the roadside can be forsaken for a path that keeps company with the beck down to near Low Bridge.

Anyone with a lust for wilderness could pick out a route further north than Nine Standards, around South Stainmore to Tan Hill, thence following the Pennine Way down into Keld.

Leave the Market Place outside the church by the short lane past the toilets, descending Stoneshot and cutting down a snicket to cross the Eden at Frank's Bridge. Turn right with the river only as far as a bend, and from the kissing-gate take a wallside path away from the river. It runs on to join the road through Hartley. Go right, the road turning to climb steeply past the awe-inspiring vastness of Hartley Quarry.

Frank's Bridge

Hartley

83

former railway

The railway through Hartley was the old Tebay-Darlington branch (again)

Kirkby Stephen

River Eden

dismantled viaduct

Hartley Quarry

Hartley Beck

The RIVER EDEN is the principal watercourse of the Lake Counties, rising on the Yorkshire border in the bleak hills of Mallerstang but rapidly broadening to thread a regal course through its pastoral vale, eventually entering the Solway Firth beyond Carlisle.

It will quickly be ascertained that Hartley Quarry is very much active. Its presence may well have been discerned several miles before Kirkby Stephen.

KIRKBY STEPHEN is small, tiny even as towns go, but in the heart of a vast rural area its importance is far greater. Its market charter was granted in 1351, and today the Market Place remains the heart of things. Characterful buildings group around, with the church of St. Stephen, dating in parts from the mid-13th century, stood behind the 'cloister'. Like Shap before it, Kirkby Stephen clings to its main road, and displays little width. A useful feature is a welcoming number of cafes.

REETH. SWALEDALE 22M.0 FUR
TO HAWES 16M.3 FUR

TO SEDBERGH 14M.0 FUR
KENDAL 23M.0 FUR

APPLEBY 12M.2 FUR
TO BROUGH 4M.3 FUR

Old roadsign preserved in Kirkby Stephen

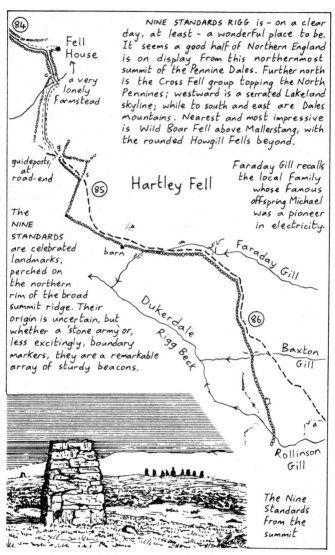

NINE STANDARDS RIGG is - on a clear day, at least - a wonderful place to be. It seems a good half of Northern England is on display from this northernmost summit of the Pennine Dales. Further north is the Cross Fell group topping the North Pennines; westward is a serrated Lakeland skyline; while to south and east are Dales mountains. Nearest and most impressive is Wild Boar Fell above Mallerstang, with the rounded Howgill Fells beyond.

⑧④

Fell House

a very lonely Farmstead

guideposts, at road-end

⑧⑤

Hartley Fell

Faraday Gill recalls the local family whose famous offspring Michael was a pioneer in electricity.

The NINE STANDARDS are celebrated landmarks, perched on the northern rim of the broad summit ridge. Their origin is uncertain, but whether a 'stone army' or, less excitingly, boundary markers, they are a remarkable array of sturdy beacons.

barn

Faraday Gill

Dukerdale

Rigg Beck

⑧⑥

Baxton Gill

Rollinson Gill

The Nine Standards from the summit

Sanity returns as the remarkably long-surfaced fell lane climbs between green verges, eventually levelling out at the isolated farmstead of Fell House. It runs on still further to a demise at a fork, where the left branch rises through a gate and onto Hartley Fell. Continuing as a broad track - with the Nine Standards intermittently in view - it remains infallible until, after leaving the wall behind, it rises above a ruinous shelter-cairn up to the foot of the peat hags that decorate the upper contours of Nine Standards Rigg. Beyond long-abandoned coal pits a single path continues, occasionally cairned as it works through the hags defending the summit. Fear not, this is hardly Kinder, and the Ordnance column should be attained without undue discomfort.

A little to the north are the Standards themselves, reached by a path passing a view indicator en route. The walk, however, continues by heading south, past a delicately sharp cairn and adjacent shelter and on through more modest groughs before a minor rise to White Mossy Hill, marked only by the odd stone. The well-worn path continues a gradual descent towards Swaledale, with Birkdale Tarn ahead and the heights of Rogan's Seat and Great Shunner Fell hemming in the upper dale.

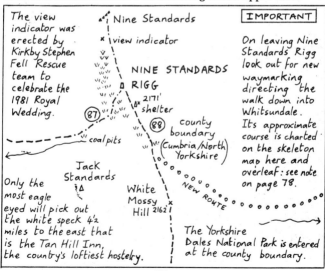

The view indicator was erected by Kirkby Stephen Fell Rescue team to celebrate the 1981 Royal Wedding.

Nine Standards

x view indicator

NINE STANDARDS RIGG

2171'

shelter

(87)

(88) county boundary

coal pits

(Cumbria/North Yorkshire)

Jack Standards

White Mossy Hill 2162'

NEW ROUTE

Only the most eagle eyed will pick out the white speck 4½ miles to the east that is the Tan Hill Inn, the country's loftiest hostelry.

IMPORTANT

On leaving Nine Standards Rigg look out for new waymarking directing the walk down into Whitsundale. Its approximate course is charted on the skeleton map here and overleaf: see note on page 78.

The Yorkshire Dales National Park is entered at the county boundary.

77

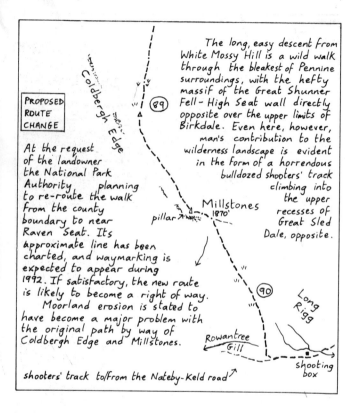

The long, easy descent from White Mossy Hill is a wild walk through the bleakest of Pennine surroundings, with the hefty massif of the Great Shunner Fell - High Seat wall directly opposite over the upper limits of Birkdale. Even here, however, man's contribution to the wilderness landscape is evident in the form of a horrendous bulldozed shooters' track climbing into the upper recesses of Great Sled Dale, opposite.

PROPOSED ROUTE CHANGE

At the request of the landowner the National Park Authority planning to re-route the walk from the county boundary to near Raven Seat. Its approximate line has been charted, and waymarking is expected to appear during 1992. If satisfactory, the new route is likely to become a right of way.

Moorland erosion is stated to have become a major problem with the original path by way of Coldbergh Edge and Millstones.

Coldbergh Edge

89

Millstones 1870'

pillar

90

Long Rigg

Rowantree Gill

shooting box

shooters' track to/from the Nateby-Keld road

Beyond a shelter, a prominent pillar on the boulders of Millstones makes an obvious halting place before the path - damp at times - moves pleasantly on down to intercept a shooters' track. Its hard surface is followed left only as far as the hut it serves, from where a more accommodating footpath takes up the running. The stream of Ney Gill provides company, and is briefly crossed at one point as a fence and an old wall nudge us off course. When a wall crosses the beck so do we, rising to follow the wall around to drop down onto the cul-de-sac road into Raven Seat.

At Raven Seat

APPROXIMATE LINE OF PROPOSED NEW ROUTE

The Swale, whose headwaters we are entering, is formed by the meeting of Birkdale (shadowed by the Nateby road) and neighbouring Great Sled Dale. The new river is soon effectively doubled in power on absorbing the waters of Whitsundale Beck.

Raven Seat

Whitsundale Beck

91

fold

Ney Gill

grouse butts

92

to B6270

Cross the cattle-grid into the farming hamlet, and after crossing the shapely bridge turn immediately up to the house on the right. In its yard a gate on the right sets a course that runs along the opposite bank, parallel with Whitsundale Beck.

From a gate just above an attractive waterfall climb half-left to a barn, thence continuing on a higher level through the pastures above the superb and unexpected scenery of How Edge Scars and Oven Mouth. Beyond a gate in a fence the path forks: take the right one to pass along the base of a large crumbling enclosure. Continue on the level trod beyond, bearing left above the barns of Smithy Holme to arrive at a gate in the corner. A good track now drops past a farm and down towards the Kirkby Stephen-Keld road at Low Bridge.

After a gate before the final drop however, go left along the top of a crumbled wall, to commence a level march along the unseen crest of the wooded top of Cotterby Scar. Wainwath Force is seen below as the path turns to descend to the Tan Hill road, on a bend just above its junction with the valley road. Go down it to the bridge over the Swale and turn left for Keld, on what remains one of the longest quarter-miles in the North.

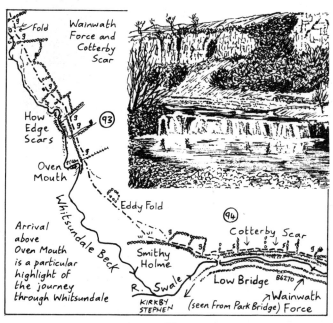

Wainwath Force and Cotterby Scar

Fold

How Edge Scars

93

Oven Mouth

Eddy Fold

94

Cotterby Scar

Whitsundale Beck

Arrival above Oven Mouth is a particular highlight of the journey through Whitsundale

Smithy Holme

R. Swale

KIRKBY STEPHEN

Low Bridge   B6270

(seen from Park Bridge)

Wainwath Force

Kisdon Force, Keld

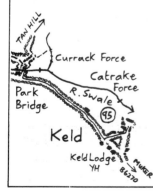

KELD is the first outpost of any size in Swaledale, and is a welcoming apparition in our descent from the high country. The heart of this old Norse settlement is found grouped around a sloping square, below the main road but high above the Swale. Its hostelry the 'Cat Hole Inn' long since called time, though as meeting place of Coast to Coast and Pennine Way, it would more than likely pay its way today. Unchanged, however, are the waterfalls, and these make Keld special.

SECTION 7

KELD TO REETH

11 miles

1800 feet of ascent

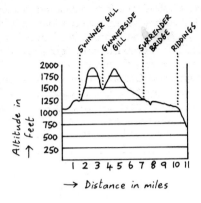

This direct march over the moors is short but time-consuming, certainly if taking any interest in the wealth of remains of a once-thriving lead industry. In the recesses of Swinner Gill, Gunnerside Gill and Hard Level Gill are the ruins of smelting mills and associated workings, while the intervening moortops still sport their vast tracts of mining debris. It's not all savage industrial wilderness however, for charming deep-cut gills and purple heather moors are interspersed, and in the latter stages the mining scenes give way entirely to the softer surrounds of Swaledale at its brilliant best.

The only unfortunate aspect of this route is that it does not more satisfyingly combine the moorland with the valley scenery, and for this reason a good many Coast to Coasters choose to take the valley option, which more than does justice to the beautiful rushing Swale. This runs an entirely different route to the main one, on a parallel course shadowing the Swale downstream. Riverside paths for the most part ensure the Swale is rarely forsaken, and even the innumerable stiles fail to compensate for the ups and downs of the moorland route. Last but not least, this enticing alternative has one - or rather several - further advantages, namely a variety of refreshment venues throughout its length.

Leave Keld by the rough lane at the side of the tiny square, soon turning left at a fork to descend to a footbridge over the Swale. The path winds up past the delectable East Gill Force, where, at a junction, the Pennine Way turns left to begin its climb to Tan Hill, and our route bears right above the fall. A broad track runs impressively above the Swale Gorge, rising left at a fork to the remains of Crackpot Hall. Climbing behind the ruins the track runs along to a gate to enter the confines of Swinner Gill. A simple bridge crosses the beck below the ravine of Swinnergill Kirk, and the path turns to climb past the ruin of a smelt mill and then more stiffly up alongside East Grain.

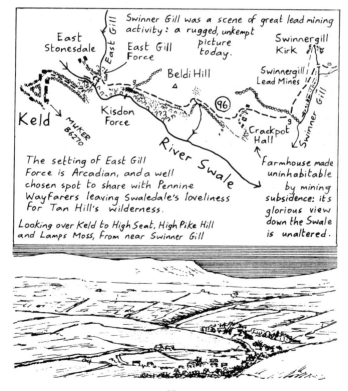

Swinner Gill was a scene of great lead mining activity: a rugged, unkempt picture today.

East Stonesdale

East Gill

East Gill Force

Swinnergill Kirk

Beldi Hill

Swinnergill Lead Mines

Keld

MUKER B6270

Kisdon Force

96

Crackpot Hall

Swinner Gill

River Swale

The setting of East Gill Force is Arcadian, and a well chosen spot to share with Pennine Wayfarers leaving Swaledale's loveliness for Tan Hill's wilderness.

Farmhouse made uninhabitable by mining subsidence: its glorious view down the Swale is unaltered.

Looking over Keld to High Seat, High Pike Hill and Lamps Moss, from near Swinner Gill

As the gradient eases, marshy ground and an old fold are encountered just before arriving at the shameless scar of another bulldozed shooters' track. This is crossed straight over but soon joined permanently to run - pleasantly, in parts - along the moortop to a junction on the very brow. A stonier continuation now leads along to overlook the valley of Gunnerside Gill. Beyond a stone fold, as the track swings to the right, a cairn indicates the departure of our footpath off to the left through heather, first running along the unfolding rim of North Hush's ravine before slanting down to the remains of Blakethwaite Smelt Mill.

Cross the slab bridge and take a short zigzag path directly behind the ruin to climb to a broad green way. Turn right along this lovely terraced pathway, with its good views down the well-wooded lower reaches of the gill, to drop down to a twin-cairned path junction above Bunton Crushing Mill. The path straight ahead runs past the mill and down the gill into Gunnerside, but our way is the broad one bearing gently left up the slope.

An option here is to climb rather strenuously up through the savagery of Bunton Hush to the moor above, though by far the gentler approach is to remain on the green track through a gateway, thence climb the grassy fellside near the crumbling wall. Below a sheepfold the wall is re-crossed by another green track, an increasingly broad and stony way then making the final pull onto the scarred moortop. This is now followed through a scene of untold devastation of the Old Gang Mines.

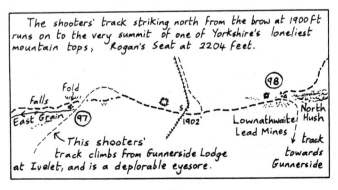

The shooters' track striking north from the brow at 1900ft runs on to the very summit of one of Yorkshire's loneliest mountain tops, Rogan's Seat at 2204 feet.

Fold
Falls
East Grain (97)
1902'
(98)
Lownathwaite
Lead Mines
North Hush
track towards Gunnerside

This shooters' track climbs from Gunnerside Lodge at Ivelet, and is a deplorable eyesore.

Blakethwaite
Smelt Mill

The lead mines and ancillary workings are as much
a part of Swaledale as the waterfalls of Keld, and this
side-valley of GUNNERSIDE GILL is an excellent venue for
their inspection. Indeed, this is probably the grandest
small valley in the whole of the Dales.

Our main interest is with the Blakethwaite Smelt Mill,
which was built around 1820 to serve the mines on the
moors above. Best surviving feature is the peat store, its
ruinous form looking equally at home at Shap or Mount
Grace. On the descent to and climb from the gill, the
main eye-catching features are the hushes, created
by the release of previously dammed
up water which tore away the
hillside in the constant search
for workable veins.

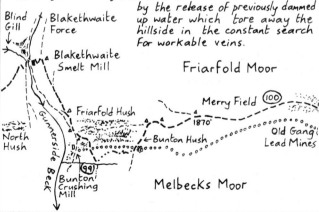

Blind Gill

Blakethwaite Force

Blakethwaite Smelt Mill

Friarfold Moor

North Hush

Gunnerside Beck

Friarfold Hush

Merry Field (100)

1870

Bunton Hush

Old Gang Lead Mines

(99)

Bunton Crushing Mill

Melbecks Moor

The track gradually drops to meet Hard Level Gill at Level House Bridge, continuing down the side of the beck past the evocative remains of the Old Gang Smelt Mill and down to a moorland road at Surrender Bridge.

Cross straight over the road and away along a clear path, passing above the Surrender Smelt Mill and on through heather to negotiate a crossing of the steep-walled Cringley Bottom. A stile on the wall at the other side precedes a much steadier jaunt on an increasingly clear track, with the profile of Calver Hill directly in front.

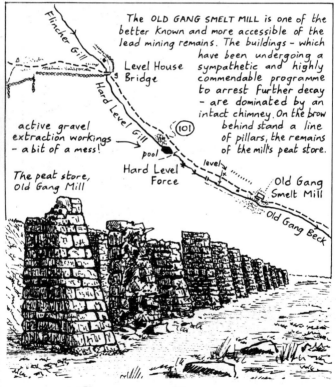

Flincher Gill

Hard Level Gill

Level House Bridge

(101)

pool

Hard Level Force

active gravel extraction workings – a bit of a mess!

The peat store, Old Gang Mill

The OLD GANG SMELT MILL is one of the better known and more accessible of the lead mining remains. The buildings – which have been undergoing a sympathetic and highly commendable programme to arrest further decay – are dominated by an intact chimney. On the brow behind stand a line of pillars, the remains of the mill's peat store.

level

Old Gang Smelt Mill

Old Gang Beck

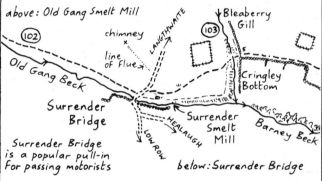

above: Old Gang Smelt Mill

chimney

line of flue

102

Old Gang Beck

LANGTHWAITE

↓Bleaberry Gill

103

Cringley Bottom

Surrender Bridge

Surrender Smelt Mill

Barney Beck

LOW ROW

HEALAUGH

Surrender Bridge is a popular pull-in for passing motorists

below: Surrender Bridge

The Surrender Smelt Mill, stands only yards down from the bridge, and is also worthy of careful inspection. On the crossing to Cringley Bottom there are good views down the heavily wooded Barney Beck.

Calver Hill

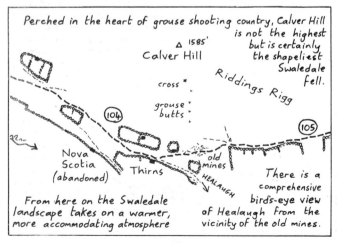

Perched in the heart of grouse shooting country, Calver Hill is not the highest but is certainly the shapeliest Swaledale fell.

△ 1585'
Calver Hill

Riddings Rigg

cross *

grouse
butts *

(104)

(105)

Nova
Scotia
(abandoned)

Thirns

old
mines

HEALAUGH

There is a
comprehensive
bird's-eye view
of Healaugh from the
vicinity of the old mines.

From here on the Swaledale
landscape takes on a warmer,
more accommodating atmosphere

The track runs along to the farm buildings of Thirns, whose access road descends to Healaugh. Attractive as it is, it has nothing to tempt us, so branch left on a rough track climbing steeply to a cottage (Moorcock) before continuing up through old mine workings to find level ground. Calver Hill is immediately above now as the path runs across the moor, largely with a wall for company.

Above the farm of Riddings remain on the path across the moor to the next wall-corner, behind which a hidden green way known as Skelgate waits to deliver you into Reeth. Its enchanting start is soon overtaken by rather exuberant undergrowth, and whilst a riot of colour it is not ideal in shorts. Just past a clearing take a stile by a gate on the right, and escape down the fields to a short snicket onto the valley road alongside the village school on the edge of Reeth.

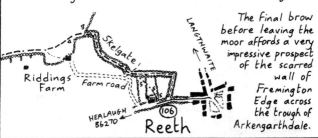

REETH is the proud capital of Swaledale, boasting an enviable position on the lower slopes of Calver Hill. Sat high above the confluence of Arkle Beck with the Swale, it shows greater allegiance to the former, leaving neighbouring Grinton to claim the Swale. The village centrepiece is a large, sloping green, with all buildings of importance stood respectfully back.

This one-time market town has a confident air about it, radiating largely from the hoary inns and shops, high-storeyed buildings alongside the green. Reeth caters indiscriminately for dalesfolk and visitors alike, though in the lead mining days of the last century it would have been far more populous. There is an absorbing folk museum here, while agricultural shows and festivals add to the cultural attractions.

On leaving Reeth, most visitors will vow to return again.

The final brow before leaving the moor affords a very impressive prospect of the scarred wall of Fremington Edge across the trough of Arkengarthdale.

Riddings Farm   Farm road   Skelgate   LANGTHWAITE

HEALAUGH B6270   106   Reeth

SECTION 8

REETH TO RICHMOND

11 miles

900 feet of ascent

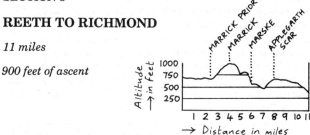

The easiest of the twelve sections has been neatly incorporated in order to leave time to explore Richmond, though in truth one could easily set a whole day aside for that purpose. Encompassed within these few miles is an old priory, a couple of lovely villages, and a range of natural scenery from limestone scars and woodland to lush fields and leafy becks. The only wonder is why the original route let the lovely riverside section by Grinton Bridge slip the net: it's there to enjoy, and makes a far pleasanter start to the day.

If wanting to lengthen the day, then consider going north from Reeth Bridge to Fremington Edge, and across through Hurst and Washfold to the head of the Marske valley. A walk down this verdant vale picks up the main route again in the village, while a further departure from it would be for a riverside path that drops down from Applegarth and culminates on the opposite bank at Richmond Bridge.

Marske Hall

Leave Reeth by the Richmond road at the bottom of the green, and on crossing Reeth Bridge, look for a wicket-gate on the right. After passing alongside a farm, the path short-cuts Arkle Beck's confluence with the Swale by bearing across to a wall-corner, rounding it to a wicket-gate and aiming for Grinton Bridge. Grinton village is over the bridge, but our route only crosses the Reeth-Grinton road, where a footpath clings to the riverbank until deflected up through a pocket wood onto the surfaced lane to Marrick Priory.

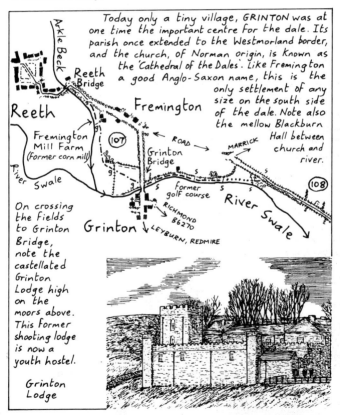

Arkle Beck

Reeth Bridge

Reeth

Fremington

Fremington Mill Farm (former corn mill)

107

River Swale

Grinton Bridge

ROAD

MARRICK

108

former golf course

River Swale

On crossing the fields to Grinton Bridge, note the castellated Grinton Lodge high on the moors above. This former shooting lodge is now a youth hostel.

Grinton

RICHMOND B6270

LEYBURN, REDMIRE

Today only a tiny village, GRINTON was at one time the important centre for the dale. Its parish once extended to the Westmorland border, and the church, of Norman origin, is known as the 'Cathedral of the Dales'. Like Fremington a good Anglo-Saxon name, this is the only settlement of any size on the south side of the dale. Note also the mellow Blackburn Hall between church and river.

Grinton Lodge

91

At the priory cross the cattle-grid and leave the farm road by a gate on the left, a short path leading to a gate into Steps Wood. A splendid flagged path climbs through it, the way remaining obvious to continue up to emerge as a lane into Marrick. Bear right at the junction, running along to then swing left up to a junction by the phone box. Go right here (noting the sundial) to yet another junction, and take the cul-de-sac lane to the right, curving round to an early demise just past the old school. Turn left up past the adjacent house on a short-lived green way that terminates at the first of many stiles in quick succession. The easternmost habitations of Marrick are skirted, passing a group of sheds and continuing on to a stile into a damp enclosure. At the far end things become easier, a thin path crossing meadows to descend to a farm track near Nun Cote Nook.

Use it only to pass through the gate before turning down the field to a barn, the thin path then continuing down to Ellers. Cross the footbridge on its far side and slant up the next two fields to join the farm road to Hollins. Turn right towards the farm, but without entering its confines turn left to a stile just above the tiny wood. Slant up the next field to the top corner, continuing on a short way to a gate on the right, there crossing the brow to slant down to a stile onto a road. Turn down to the right for a long descent to Marske, in view well in advance of arrival there.

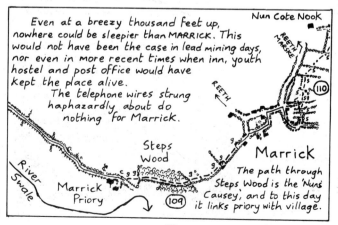

Even at a breezy thousand feet up, nowhere could be sleepier than MARRICK. This would not have been the case in lead mining days, nor even in more recent times when inn, youth hostel and post office would have kept the place alive.

The telephone wires strung haphazardly about do nothing for Marrick.

Nun Cote Nook

REETH MARSKE

REETH

110

Steps Wood

River Swale

Marrick Priory

109

Marrick

The path through Steps Wood is the 'Nuns' Causey', and to this day it links priory with village.

On emerging onto the lane beyond Hollins, a sign warns of 'bulls in field on path to Marrick'. The suggestion of an 'alternative route by road' is a) a damn cheek and b) a fat lot of use to us now. On a brighter note, in front is the verdant upper valley of Marske Beck, a lovely sight.

Hutton's Monument recalls Matthew Hutton, a member of the once influential family of Marske Hall.

The idyllic setting of the house at Ellers remains as inaccessible as when observed by Wainwright.

Marske

SKELTON

Hall

112

REETH

this is the old main Reeth-Richmond highway

Hutton's Monument

Hollins Farm

Ellers Beck

111

Ellers

MARRICK PRIORY was founded in its pastoral Swaledale setting early in the 12th century to accommodate Benedictine nuns. The remains – of which the tower dominates – have been incorporated into a residential youth activity centre: visitors are welcome to have a look around the grounds.

The Farm adjacent to the priory is named Abbey Farm

Marrick Priory

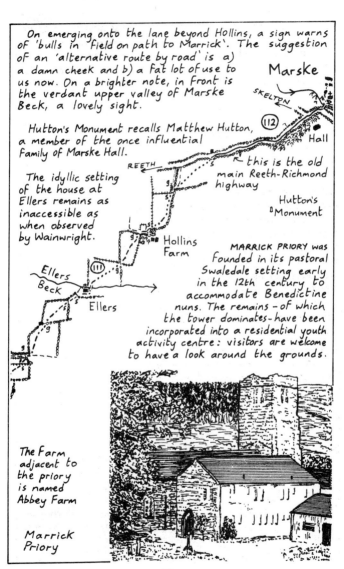

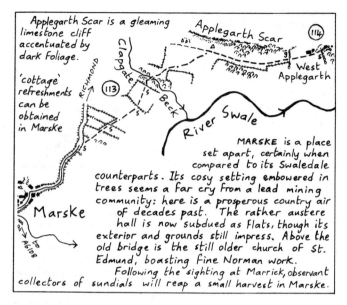

Applegarth Scar is a gleaming limestone cliff accentuated by dark foliage.

'cottage' refreshments can be obtained in Marske

Applegarth Scar

West Applegarth

RICHMOND

Clapgate Beck

(113)

River Swale

Marske

A6108

MARSKE is a place set apart, certainly when compared to its Swaledale counterparts. Its cosy setting embowered in trees seems a far cry from a lead mining community: here is a prosperous country air of decades past. The rather austere hall is now subdued as Flats, though its exterior and grounds still impress. Above the old bridge is the still older church of St. Edmund, boasting fine Norman work.

Following the sighting at Marrick, observant collectors of sundials will reap a small harvest in Marske.

Cross Marske Bridge and rise up past the church to a junction, going right as far as the second bend in the road. Here a sign points the way through a string of hedges before the thin path drops down to a bridge over Clapgate Beck. A clear path slants up the opposite slope to a beckoning cairn alongside a farm road. Follow it right to West Applegarth and keep straight on to a barn beyond it. A stile leads on past the barn and across to another stile, from where a field is crossed to emerge on the drive to Low Applegarth Farm.

Cross straight over this to the next stile, and on further near the front of High Applegarth (a barn conversion) and on to the road serving East Applegarth. This is left, however, even before the farm's barns are reached, as a stile on the left points the way across a pasture well above the farm. At a stile above it, a clearer path runs on to meet a cart-track rising from the farm, and this is followed undulatingly through rougher country to enter Whitcliffe Wood and re-emerge on the other side.

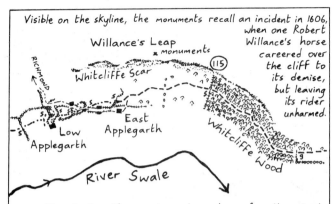

Visible on the skyline, the monuments recall an incident in 1606, when one Robert Willance's horse careered over the cliff to its demise, but leaving its rider unharmed.

The Applegarth area is quite a haven from the outside world. Its string of farms is sat on a green ledge beneath the scars and high above the Swale. The only road in is the narrow access road snaking down from the old Reeth - Richmond coach road. Here, between West and Low Applegarth, we vacate the Yorkshire Dales National Park. The profusion of 'no public right of way' notices in the vicinity is quite unique.

East Applegarth

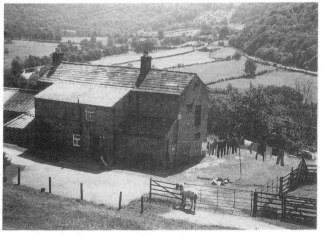

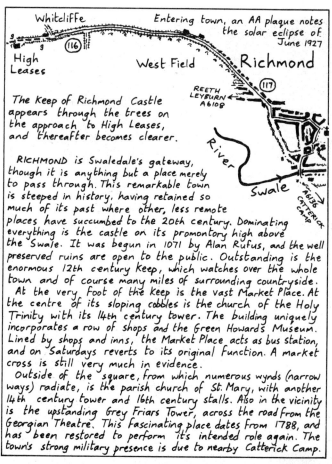

Whitcliffe

Entering town, an AA plaque notes the solar eclipse of June 1927

High Leases

West Field

Richmond

REETH
LEYBURN ←
A6108

The Keep of Richmond Castle appears through the trees on the approach to High Leases, and thereafter becomes clearer.

River

Swale

CATTERICK CAMP
A6136

RICHMOND is Swaledale's gateway, though it is anything but a place merely to pass through. This remarkable town is steeped in history, having retained so much of its past where other, less remote places have succumbed to the 20th century. Dominating everything is the castle on its promontory high above the Swale. It was begun in 1071 by Alan Rufus, and the well preserved ruins are open to the public. Outstanding is the enormous 12th century keep, which watches over the whole town and of course many miles of surrounding countryside.

At the very foot of the keep is the vast Market Place. At the centre of its sloping cobbles is the church of the Holy Trinity with its 14th century tower. The building uniquely incorporates a row of shops and the Green Howards Museum. Lined by shops and inns, the Market Place acts as bus station, and on Saturdays reverts to its original function. A market cross is still very much in evidence.

Outside of the square, from which numerous wynds (narrow ways) radiate, is the parish church of St. Mary, with another 14th century tower and 16th century stalls. Also in the vicinity is the upstanding Grey Friars Tower, across the road from the Georgian Theatre. This fascinating place dates from 1788, and has been restored to perform its intended role again. The town's strong military presence is due to nearby Catterick Camp.

The track runs on past High Leases, soon becoming surfaced for a long approach descent into Richmond. Above the public place of West Field one can squeeze through one of several stiles to follow a path along its top, either returning to Westfields to descend past a nice string of houses, or dropping to the bottom corner of the field to meet the road at the edge of town.

Richmond Castle from the Swale

SECTION 9

RICHMOND TO INGLEBY CROSS

23 miles   *500 feet of ascent*

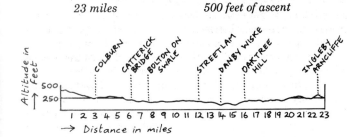

The longest section on offer, this near-marathon crossing of the Vale of Mowbray gets you from the Dales to the Moors in one fell swoop, a worthy objective if you've a liking for elevated ground. Certainly there are features of interest, though if this is all for one day then you don't want too many distractions. The Swale itself provides early company, while there are moments to break the monotony at Bolton on Swale and Danby Wiske.

Although the amount of road walking is a little less than it once was, there are nevertheless a good few miles of tarmac bashing. The advantages, however, are several: faster progress is a major one, for if gobbling all this up in one day, then the likelihood is that paths around three sides of a cornfield and such like would only be abandoned in order to maintain a reasonable bee-line; the roads are in any case virtually traffic-free; one should be in reasonable shape if the previous day was only the suggested stroll from Reeth.

Options to shorten the walking are naturally few, though one could get off to a flyer by eschewing the intricate early miles in favour of a route by way of Easby Abbey and Brompton on Swale, mapped on the following pages; certainly Easby Abbey and its lovely environs deserve a visit. An obvious little short-cut from Danby Lane to Oaktree Hill was, at the time of writing, largely impassable. If bound for Osmotherley, one could significantly shorten things by leaving Long Lane in favour of a route by Low Moor and Harlsey Castle.

From the Market Place's south-west corner descend charming streets to cross Castle Bridge. Follow the Swale downstream into woodland, the path soon rising to a field. Go left and locate a stile on the right, as the more obvious way runs on towards Station Bridge: our path rises between barns to run along the front of a row of houses. At the main road go right, and when it swings right, take a tarmac road doubling back to the left. At the sewage works the path bears right to run outside its boundary.

On entering woodland the way soon forks, the lower one being less muddy. Merging at a footbridge, the path climbs to the wood-top and along to a stile, escaping to reach ruinous Hagg Farm. A track heads away, and at a gateway fades as a thin, clear trod rises across the field. Continue over the brow in the next field to a stile at the far corner, then descend a field-side.

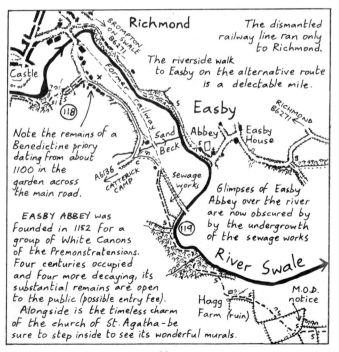

Richmond

BROMPTON ON SWALE B6271

The dismantled railway line ran only to Richmond.

Castle

The riverside walk to Easby on the alternative route is a delectable mile.

Former railway

118

Easby

RICHMOND B6271

Note the remains of a Benedictine priory dating from about 1100 in the garden across the main road.

Sand Beck

Abbey

Easby House

A6136 CATTERICK CAMP

sewage works

EASBY ABBEY was founded in 1152 for a group of White Canons of the Premonstratensians. Four centuries occupied and four more decaying, its substantial remains are open to the public (possible entry fee). Alongside is the timeless charm of the church of St. Agatha - be sure to step inside to see its wonderful murals.

119

Glimpses of Easby Abbey over the river are now obscured by by the undergrowth of the sewage works

River Swale

Hagg Farm (ruin)

M.O.D. notice

99

The Swale at Catterick Bridge

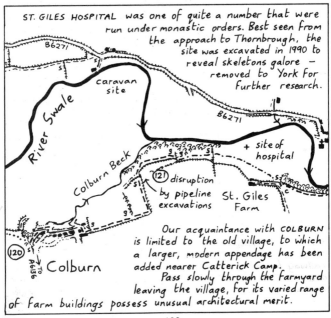

ST. GILES HOSPITAL was one of quite a number that were run under monastic orders. Best seen from the approach to Thornbrough, the site was excavated in 1990 to reveal skeletons galore — removed to York for further research.

B6271

caravan site

River Swale

B6271

Colburn Beck

(121) disruption by pipeline excavations

+ site of hospital

St. Giles Farm

(120)

→ TO A6136

Colburn

Our acquaintance with COLBURN is limited to the old village, to which a larger, modern appendage has been added nearer Catterick Camp.

Pass slowly through the farmyard leaving the village, for its varied range of farm buildings possess unusual architectural merit.

Down the field bear slightly right to locate a part-hidden stile into the trees. A clear path now accompanies a small beck to emerge onto a drive, there turning right to enter sleepy Colburn.

Cross the road bridge almost opposite and head along the street past the inn. At the end go straight ahead, turning sharp right into a farmyard, then left along a cart-track. At its far end it turns left to continue high above a wooded bank of the river: ahead, waggons stream over the Swale on the modern A1 bridge. Two gates convey the way on, rising gradually to bypass St Giles Farm and emerge onto its drive. Almost at once however, go left after a cattle-grid with a fence above a wooded bank, and from a stile at the end head on to join a cart-track along the bank top to Thornbrough. Again without disturbing the farm, drop left to discover the A1 just below!

Pass under this and a defunct railway bridge to rise slightly right to a stile onto the old A1 opposite the racecourse. Go left past the hotel and cross the bridge with care. Immediately over take a stile on the right to follow the riverbank, a generally clear path accompanying either the Swale itself or, for a time, a crumbling wall alongside a scrubby area.

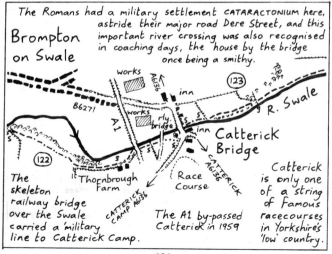

The Romans had a military settlement CATARACTONIUM here, astride their major road Dere Street, and this important river crossing was also recognised in coaching days, the house by the bridge once being a smithy.

Brompton on Swale

works

A6136

123

inn

B6271

A1

works

rly. bridge

inn

R. Swale

Catterick Bridge

122

Thornbrough Farm

CATTERICK CAMP A6136

Race Course

CATTERICK A6136

The skeleton railway bridge over the Swale carried a military line to Catterick Camp.

The A1 by-passed Catterick in 1959

Catterick is only one of a string of famous racecourses in Yorkshire's 'low' country.

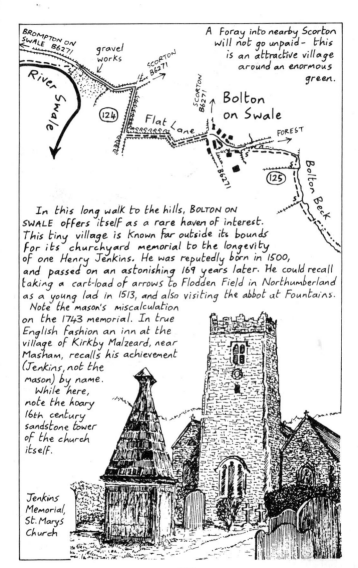

A foray into nearby Scorton will not go unpaid– this is an attractive village around an enormous green.

BROMPTON ON SWALE B6271

gravel works

SCORTON B6271

River Swale

124

Flat Lane

SCORTON B6271

Bolton on Swale

FOREST

B6271

125

Bolton Beck

In this long walk to the hills, BOLTON ON SWALE offers itself as a rare haven of interest. This tiny village is known far outside its bounds for its churchyard memorial to the longevity of one Henry Jenkins. He was reputedly born in 1500, and passed on an astonishing 169 years later. He could recall taking a cart-load of arrows to Flodden Field in Northumberland as a young lad in 1513, and also visiting the abbot at Fountains.

Note the mason's miscalculation on the 1743 memorial. In true English fashion an inn at the village of Kirkby Malzeard, near Masham, recalls his achievement (Jenkins, not the mason) by name.

While here, note the hoary 16th century sandstone tower of the church itself.

Jenkins Memorial, St. Mary's Church

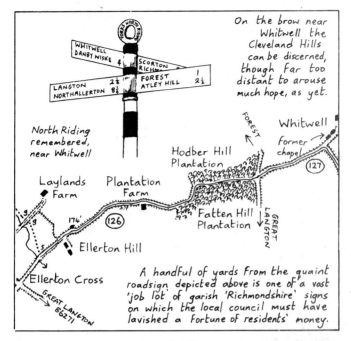

On the brow near Whitwell the Cleveland Hills can be discerned, though far too distant to arouse much hope, as yet.

WHITWELL DANBY WISKE 4

SCORTON RICHM

LANGTON 2½ NORTHALLERTON 8½

FOREST ATLEY HILL 1 2½

North Riding remembered, near Whitwell

FOREST

Whitwell

former chapel

127

Hodber Hill Plantation

Laylands Farm

Plantation Farm

Fatten Hill Plantation

GREAT LANGTON

174'

126

Ellerton Hill

Ellerton Cross

GREAT LANGTON B6271

A handful of yards from the quaint roadsign depicted above is one of a vast 'job lot' of garish 'Richmondshire' signs on which the local council must have lavished a fortune of residents' money.

On approaching a gravel works the pleasant riverbank path slants across a long field up onto the B6271. Go right a short way until at the first chance turn down a lane on the right (the houses ahead belong to Catterick village, across the river). Again at the first chance, turn left along a rough lane to emerge back onto the B6271 at Bolton on Swale. Cross straight over and head for the church, passing the preserved village pump en route.

At the church bear left along the lane, and at an early stile bear left across the fields, accompanying a charming streamlet meandering through the field. At the far corner the beck-side is traced up to a crumbling stone bridge - a pleasing setting for a snack - crossing it and continuing upstream across a farm drive and along to a stile onto a lane at Ellerton Hill. This same road is now followed all the way to Streetlam, enjoying a spell amidst plantations and generally traffic-free rapid progress.

A name on the OS map just north of Streetlam conjures up a vision of everything we're missing, for despite its wilder connotations, FELL GILL MOOR promises all and delivers nowt.

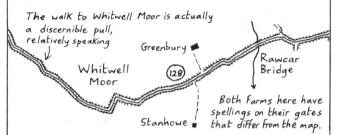

The walk to Whitwell Moor is actually a discernible pull, relatively speaking

Whitwell Moor

Greenbury

128

Rawcar Bridge

Stanhowe

Both Farms here have spellings on their gates that differ from the map.

DANBY WISKE has earned for itself a modest reputation as the only staging post on the long haul to Ingleby Cross. It is the most peaceful of communities, though the sight of booted legions striding through is no longer a bizarre apparition to its residents. Indeed, Danby Wiske is a veritable haven, with the opportunity for a pint on the green, or, on the outskirts, tea on the lawn. It may well be the lowest point between the two seashores, but it certainly does its best.

Just down the lane is its attractive church, which incorporates work from many periods, all the way back to Norman origins.

At Danby Wiske

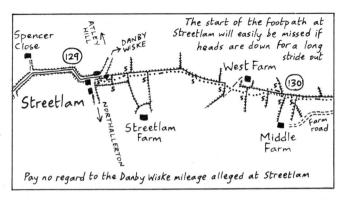

The start of the footpath at Streetlam will easily be missed if heads are down for a long stride out

Spencer Close

ATLEY HILL

DANBY WISKE

129

Streetlam

NORTHALLERTON

Streetlam Farm

West Farm

130

Middle Farm

farm road

Pay no regard to the Danby Wiske mileage alleged at Streetlam

At the road junction in Streetlam an obvious improvement to the original route awaits in the form of a respite from the tarmac. Just on the corner is a stile, for a direct line treks across numerous fields, beyond the initial paddocks the way simply keeping to the left-hand field boundary. It's marginally shorter if no quicker, but is gentler on the feet. At the other end a farm road is joined to lead back onto the original lane, now just minutes out of Danby Wiske, descending Park Hill into the village. With these miles of tarmac the warning of 'no footway for 400 yards' should not be taken too seriously.

Leave Danby by keeping straight on the road, bridging the snaking Wiske and, a little beyond, the railway line.

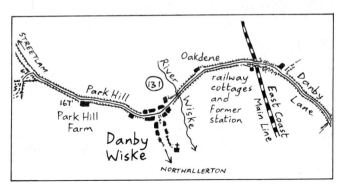

STREETLAM

Oakdene

River Wiske

Park Hill

131

railway cottages and former station

Danby Lane

East Coast Main Line

167'

Park Hill Farm

Danby Wiske

NORTHALLERTON

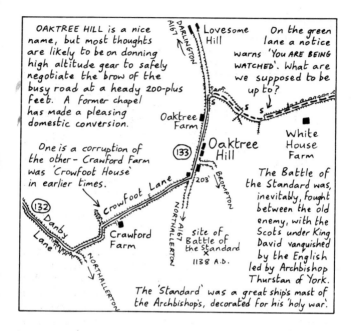

OAKTREE HILL is a nice name, but most thoughts are likely to be on donning high altitude gear to safely negotiate the brow of the busy road at a heady 200-plus feet. A former chapel has made a pleasing domestic conversion.

One is a corruption of the other - Crawford Farm was 'Crowfoot House' in earlier times.

Lovesome Hill

On the green lane a notice warns 'YOU ARE BEING WATCHED'. What are we supposed to be up to?

Oaktree Farm

White House Farm

Oaktree Hill

The Battle of the Standard was, inevitably, fought between the old enemy, with the Scots under King David vanquished by the English led by Archbishop Thurstan of York.

Crowfoot Lane

Danby Lane

Crawford Farm

site of Battle of the Standard ✕ 1138 A.D.

The 'Standard' was a great ship's mast of the Archbishop's, decorated for his 'holy war'.

Remain on Danby Lane as far as a junction, turning left to zigzag along to meet the pulsating A167 at Oaktree Hill. Cross when possible to the Oak Tree Garage, and if not interested in a rusting FSO, keep straight on past Oak Tree Farm (opposite) to escape by a stile on the right. A broad green haven heads away, soon becoming (too) enclosed, but gradually broadening to emerge onto Deighton Lane.

Go left only as far as a drive branching right to Moor House Farm. Keep straight on between the buildings to a gate, and across a field to cross a tiny stream. Go half-left passing near the ruin of Brompton Moor Farm to the far corner, then run along to another streamlet before the path strikes directly ahead for the hotchpotch of buildings of Northfield Farm. Keep left of them all to a stile, then straight ahead to the next stile to join the farm road. Go left past Northfield House and out onto another road.

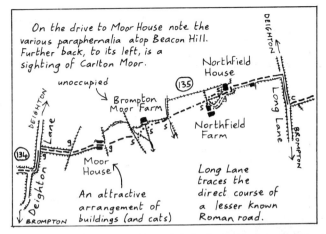

On the drive to Moor House note the various paraphernalia atop Beacon Hill. Further back, to its left, is a sighting of Carlton Moor.

unoccupied

Brompton Moor Farm

DEIGHTON

135

Northfield House

Northfield Farm

Long Lane

BROMPTON

DEIGHTON

134

Deighton Lane

Moor House

BROMPTON

Moor House ↖

An attractive arrangement of buildings (and cats)

Long Lane traces the direct course of a lesser known Roman road.

Turn briefly right then branch left along the drive to Wray House. Once again neatly avoiding a farmyard, go right down a short-lived way to debouch into a field with a railway ahead. Bear well to the left to a crossing, then head straight down the cornfield to a footbridge and then a plank in a field corner. Its boundary is now followed left around two sides to join the surfaced Low Moor Lane. Go left to approach the farmstead of Harlsey Grove, and when it turns in to it, bear right on the rougher continuation of Low Moor Lane.

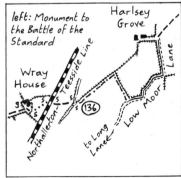

left: Monument to the Battle of the Standard

Harlsey Grove

Wray House

Northallerton - Teesside Line

136

to Long Lane

Low Moor Lane

107

A long trek along Low Moor Lane leads out to a surfaced road. Go right to the junction then left, only to turn right almost at once along the drive to Sydal Lodge. Go straight ahead at the house and on towards farm buildings, but then keep straight on again to a gate. The path heads away with the ruin of Breckon Hill a sure guide straight ahead, and the Cleveland Hills now almost touchable behind.

The path descends to a footbridge (the lazy Wiske again) and then climbs a cornfield to Breckon Hill, passing to the right of the crumbling remains to follow the drive out. The buzz of traffic on the A19 is heard as the drive zigzags past two farms to emerge onto the highway alongside a filling station and a cafe. A dual carriageway is of benefit on this final hairy crossing to a contrastingly narrow lane rising to Ingleby Arncliffe. At the staggered junction keep on to descend the road into adjacent Ingleby Cross.

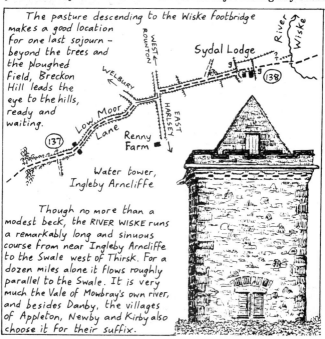

The pasture descending to the Wiske footbridge makes a good location for one last sojourn – beyond the trees and the ploughed field, Breckon Hill leads the eye to the hills, ready and waiting.

Water tower, Ingleby Arncliffe

Though no more than a modest beck, the RIVER WISKE runs a remarkably long and sinuous course from near Ingleby Arncliffe to the Swale west of Thirsk. For a dozen miles alone it flows roughly parallel to the Swale. It is very much the Vale of Mowbray's own river, and besides Danby, the villages of Appleton, Newby and Kirby also choose it for their suffix.

Above: Ingleby Cross

Breckon Hill ← a very sad ruin

Grinkle Carr

TEESSIDE

'Little Chef'

Longlands (139)

Ingleby Arncliffe

A19

THIRSK

to A19

tower

old road

STOKESLEY A172

Ingleby Cross

old road

to A19

The first sign of civilisation on entering INGLEBY ARNCLIFFE (discounting the Little Chef) might well be one hanging out of a garden announcing the availability of pansies and other pot plants — just the tonic for jaded bodies now feeling every one of those long, flat miles.

The village itself is rather attractive, the next object of note being a prominent water tower, erected by a member of the Bell family of Arncliffe Hall.

INGLEBY CROSS is the 'business' partner — now gratefully by-passed, its 'cross', its comfortable inn, its tiny post office, its village hall and all its cottages enjoy a peace disturbed only by the Northallerton–Stokesley bus and the exhausted walkers abandoned on its welcoming green.

INGLEBY CROSS

TO

CLAY BANK

TOP

12 miles

2700 feet of ascent

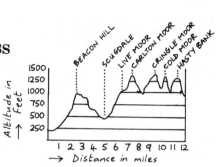

Growing ever nearer yesterday, the Cleveland Hills are now underfoot, and this is truly a day to savour, the most famous dozen miles on the North York Moors. Throughout the crossing of the escarpment are superb views not only out to the Cleveland Plain and into the heart of the moors, but also of the day's hills' ever changing aspects. Though the miles are few and the route clear, this is quite a roller-coaster. Rather than trying to press on beyond Clay Bank Top, it is recommended to take your time, include a visit to the majestic Mount Grace Priory, and finish with a downhill stroll into Great Broughton. With luck your host will even deposit you back on Clay Bank Top after breakfast.

A low level alternative exists by using lanes and field-paths north of the great escarpment, by way of Swainby, Faceby and Carlton. The route could be picked up on Carlton Bank to follow the jet miners' track (see map).

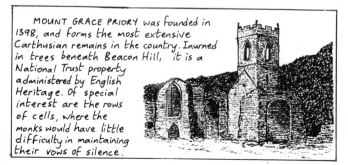

MOUNT GRACE PRIORY was founded in 1398, and forms the most extensive Carthusian remains in the country. Inurned in trees beneath Beacon Hill, it is a National Trust property administered by English Heritage. Of special interest are the rows of cells, where the monks would have little difficulty in maintaining their vows of silence.

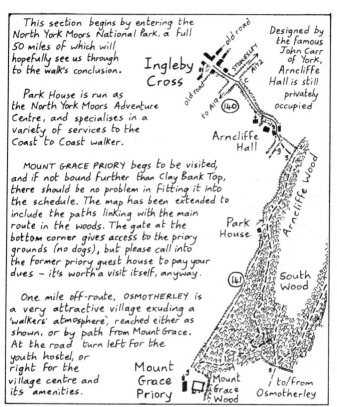

This section begins by entering the North York Moors National Park, a full 50 miles of which will hopefully see us through to the walk's conclusion.

Park House is run as the North York Moors Adventure Centre, and specialises in a variety of services to the Coast to Coast walker.

MOUNT GRACE PRIORY begs to be visited, and if not bound further than Clay Bank Top, there should be no problem in fitting it into the schedule. The map has been extended to include the paths linking with the main route in the woods. The gate at the bottom corner gives access to the priory grounds (no dogs), but please call into the former priory guest house to pay your dues – it's worth a visit itself, anyway.

One mile off-route, OSMOTHERLEY is a very attractive village exuding a 'walkers' atmosphere', reached either as shown, or by path from Mount Grace. At the road turn left for the youth hostel, or right for the village centre and its amenities.

Ingleby Cross

Designed by the famous John Carr of York, Arncliffe Hall is still privately occupied

Arncliffe Hall

Park House

Arncliffe Wood

South Wood

Mount Grace Priory

Mount Grace Wood

to/from Osmotherley

From the green head past the *Blue Bell* and out onto the A172. Cross over and head along the leafy lane past Arncliffe Church and Hall, then up the hill take a gate on the left to follow a track up to Arncliffe Wood. Turn right along the forest road, passing above Park House and then deeper into the woods. The way remains clear, swinging up to a T-junction and there rising to the right to the edge of the wood. The gate in front signals our merging with the Cleveland Way coming out from Osmotherley, but without leaving the wood turn sharply up to the left on a clear path rising through South Wood.

At the top of the wood the path runs along a wallside, past an incongruous booster station and the Ordnance column atop Beacon Hill. A little beyond, the way emerges onto a corner of Scarth Wood Moor, a glorious moment. In the distance is the conical peak of Roseberry Topping, but nearer to hand is a striking array of moors that form the greater part of the day - an exciting prospect indeed.

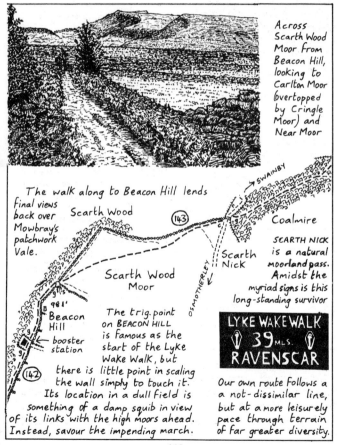

Across Scarth Wood Moor from Beacon Hill, looking to Carlton Moor (overtopped by Cringle Moor) and Near Moor

The walk along to Beacon Hill lends final views back over Mowbray's patchwork Vale.

Scarth Wood

SWAINBY

(143)

Coalmire

Scarth Nick

OSMOTHERLEY

Scarth Wood Moor

SCARTH NICK is a natural moorland pass. Amidst the myriad signs is this long-standing survivor

981'
Beacon Hill

booster station

(142)

The trig. point on BEACON HILL is famous as the start of the Lyke Wake Walk, but there is little point in scaling the wall simply to touch it. Its location in a dull field is something of a damp squib in view of its links with the high moors ahead. Instead, savour the impending march.

LYKE WAKE WALK
39 MLS.
RAVENSCAR

Our own route follows a not-dissimilar line, but at a more leisurely pace through terrain of far greater diversity.

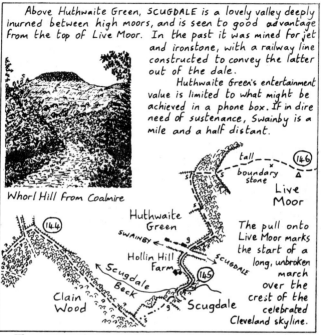

Above Huthwaite Green, SCUGDALE is a lovely valley deeply inurned between high moors, and is seen to good advantage from the top of Live Moor. In the past it was mined for jet and ironstone, with a railway line constructed to convey the latter out of the dale.

Huthwaite Green's entertainment value is limited to what might be achieved in a phone box. If in dire need of sustenance, Swainby is a mile and a half distant.

Whorl Hill from Coalmire

tall — — — 146
boundary
stone
Live
Moor

The pull onto Live Moor marks the start of a long, unbroken march over the crest of the celebrated Cleveland skyline.

Huthwaite Green
144
SWAINBY
Hollin Hill Farm
145
SCUGDALE
Scugdale Beck
Clain Wood
Scugdale

The main path crosses the moor diagonally to descend onto the road through Scarth Nick, and across the cattle-grid take a gate into the plantation. A path heads off to quickly join a forest road through Coalmire, which is left at a fork by dropping steeply to the left. At a staggered crossroads go left a couple of yards and then sharp right, a clear path running along the foot of Clain Wood. In lovely surroundings a stile on the left signals time to leave the broad path by descending a field to a rough track fording Scugdale Beck. On the other side a narrow lane leads up to the left to a junction at Huthwaite Green.

Cross straight over and up an enclosed path past the phone box, swinging left along the base of a plantation until a stile admits to a steep climb through the trees. The open moor is quickly gained, and a pleasant climb continues over the brow of Live Moor.

The summit of Carlton Moor, looking ahead to Cringle Moor

From Live Moor to CARLTON MOOR the track is visible all the way ahead, the steep western flank contrasting well with the heather carpet of the moortop. In the fashion of its ensuing colleagues, Carlton Moor rises gently from the south to an abrupt top overlooking the Cleveland Plain. Select a heathery couch and with the aid of a map, try to identify the villages outspread. The nearest, appropriately, is Carlton.

On Cringle End

Not the one of 'Hovis' advert fame → Gold Hill

1033 ▲

Live Moor

white painted boundary stone

Arrival on CRINGLE END is a champagne moment: aside from the ever-present views over the Cleveland Plain to the peak of Roseberry Topping, the highlight is the sudden appearance of Cringle's north face plunging dramatically to the lower contours, with both Cold Moor and Hasty Bank making their appearances in some style. The 'furniture' confirms this as a compulsory halt, one of those indefinable 'good places to be'.

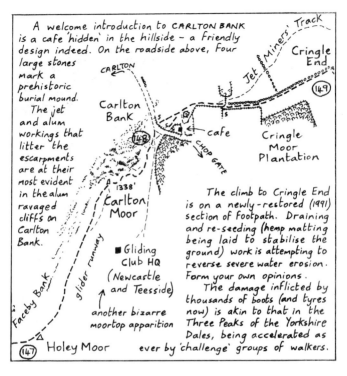

A welcome introduction to CARLTON BANK is a cafe 'hidden' in the hillside – a friendly design indeed. On the roadside above, Four large stones mark a prehistoric burial mound.

The jet and alum workings that litter the escarpments are at their most evident in the alum ravaged cliffs on Carlton Bank.

CARLTON

Jet Miners' Track

Cringle End

149

Carlton Bank

148

cafe

CHOP GATE

Cringle Moor Plantation

1338' Carlton Moor

The climb to Cringle End is on a newly-restored (1991) section of footpath. Draining and re-seeding (hemp matting being laid to stabilise the ground) work is attempting to reverse severe water erosion. Form your own opinions.

Gliding Club HQ (Newcastle and Teesside)

another bizarre moortop apparition

Faceby Bank

glider runway

147 Holey Moor

The damage inflicted by thousands of boots (and tyres now) is akin to that in the Three Peaks of the Yorkshire Dales, being accelerated as ever by 'challenge' groups of walkers.

The path runs along the crest of Live Moor and onto waiting Carlton Moor: the final section is sandwiched between the escarpment to the left and a glider runway to the right. The summit is marked by an Ordnance column and a tall boundary stone, a good place to halt. Caution is needed on the descent, where the path has been re-routed away from the precipitous drops into the alum quarries that scar the northern face of the hill. Cringle Moor waits patiently opposite, the crossing being interrupted by the Carlton-Chop Gate road on Carlton Bank.

Across the road a path runs happily along before a short pull onto Cringle End, where another boundary stone stands alongside a memorial view indicator and seat.

Cringle Moor from Cringle End,
looking to Hasty Bank, Cold Moor and the distant Urra Moor

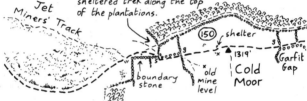

The lower-level track can be picked up in this gap for a more
sheltered trek along the top of the plantations.

Jet Miners' Track

150 shelter

boundary stone

x old mine level

1319' Cold Moor

Garfit Gap

1417' ▲ Drake Howe (tumulus)

Cringle Moor

CRINGLE MOOR is second only to Urra Moor's Round Hill in the hierarchy of the Moors, yet its summit is the only one along this escarpment that is omitted, being set well back amidst the trackless heather.

COLD MOOR points a slender finger south to Bilsdale, and from its tiny cairn a very inviting path sets off through heather.

Along with ironstone and alum, these hills were also plundered for jet (of 'jet black' fame), at one time a popular ornamental stone. Evidence of the old mines is most apparent when looking back to Cringle Moor from Cold Moor — just select the right contour.

HASTY BANK may not be the highest point on the Cleveland ridge, but it is arguably the finest. The northern scarp, in addition to its greater length, falls away in a series of superior cliffs: stride carefully here!

116

From Cringle End the path rises a little further, in dramatic fashion along the escarpment just below Cringle Moor's summit. A steep descent follows to the depression in front of Cold Moor, where a wall is followed up then crossed for the short climb to its cairn. The descent is equally rapid, spurred on by the prospect of the Wainstones on Hasty Bank, final summit before Clay Bank Top.

A short climb is followed by an easy clamber up between the pinnacles, and then a long crossing of Hasty Bank's broad top. When its northern scarp subsides, the inevitable steep descent runs down to the top of the plantations that cloak the northern slopes, and a wallside path drops the final yards onto the road.

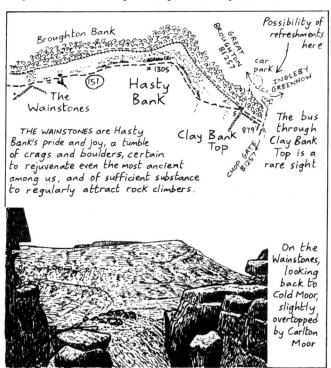

Broughton Bank

GREAT BROUGHTON B1257

Possibility of refreshments here

car park

INGLEBY GREENHOW

× 1305

(151)

The Wainstones

Hasty Bank

Clay Bank Top

879'

CHOP GATE B1257

The bus through Clay Bank Top is a rare sight

THE WAINSTONES are Hasty Bank's pride and joy, a tumble of crags and boulders, certain to rejuvenate even the most ancient among us, and of sufficient substance to regularly attract rock climbers.

On the Wainstones, looking back to Cold Moor, slightly overtopped by Carlton Moor

117

SECTION 11
CLAY BANK TOP TO GLAISDALE

18¹/₂ miles   *1000 feet of ascent*

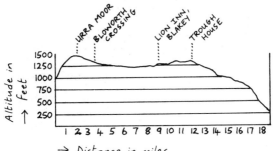

Considering that going on for a dozen miles are spent above the
1250ft contour, the walking on this section is supremely effort-
less. Only the very first half-mile pull onto Urra Moor offers any
resistance, after which broad strides, broad tracks and even
broader sweeps of moorland are the order of the day. Beyond the
summit of the moors on Round Hill, the Rosedale Ironstone
Railway trackbed is picked up at Bloworth Crossing, and winds
a well engineered course around the head of Farndale before
throwing us off at Blakey. Here the Lion Inn, only habitation of
the day, awaits our thirsts, and beyond the heart of the moors at
Rosedale Head, with its crosses and various stones, the way
resumes around the magnificent head of Great Fryup Dale, a
tributary of the Esk to which the long declining miles of Glaisdale
Rigg will lead.

No obvious alternatives present themselves, and none should
be necessary. More circuitous routes could be devised by breaking
off earlier for Eskdale, either from Bloworth to Baysdale and
thence Castleton, or down into Great Fryup Dale for Lealholm.
One could also drop south into Farndale, though this would only
be practicable if seeking a bed there.

Leave the road summit by Hagg's Gate opposite, from where a wide path rises, fairly steeply in the earlier stages, onto the heather of Urra Moor. After a mile and a half lined by innumerable cairns and boundary stones the Ordnance column on Round Hill is reached, just off to the left from the Hand Stone.

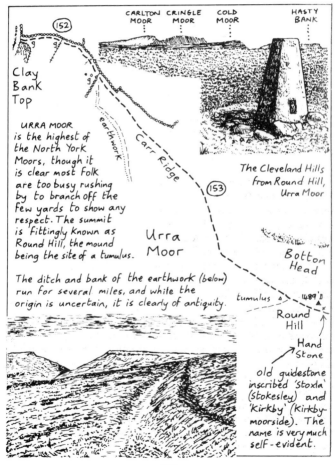

152

CARLTON MOOR CRINGLE MOOR COLD MOOR HASTY BANK

Clay Bank Top

URRA MOOR is the highest of the North York Moors, though it is clear most folk are too busy rushing by to branch off the few yards to show any respect. The summit is 'fittingly known as Round Hill, the mound being the site of a tumulus.

earthwork

Carr Ridge

153

Urra Moor

The Cleveland Hills from Round Hill, Urra Moor

Botton Head

The ditch and bank of the earthwork (below) run for several miles, and while the origin is uncertain, it is clearly of antiquity.

tumulus   1489'
Round Hill
Hand Stone

old guidestone inscribed 'Stoxla' (Stokesley) and 'Kirkby' (Kirkby-moorside). The name is very much self-evident.

119

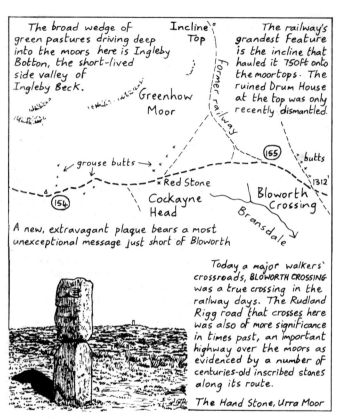

The broad wedge of green pastures driving deep into the moors here is Ingleby Botton, the short-lived side valley of Ingleby Beck.

Incline Top

The railway's grandest feature is the incline that hauled it 750ft onto the moortops. The ruined Drum House at the top was only recently dismantled.

former railway

Greenhow Moor

← grouse butts →

155

butts

Red Stone

1312'

Cockayne Head

Bloworth Crossing

154

Bransdale

A new, extravagant plaque bears a most unexceptional message just short of Bloworth

Today a major walkers' crossroads, BLOWORTH CROSSING was a true crossing in the railway days. The Rudland Rigg road that crosses here was also of more significance in times past, an important highway over the moors as evidenced by a number of centuries-old inscribed stones along its route.

The Hand Stone, Urra Moor

Beyond Round Hill the broad track makes a dignified descent to merge with the trackbed of the former Rosedale Ironstone Railway, whose course will be discerned well before it is joined. Only a little further is Bloworth Crossing, a major moorland crossroads. Here we take our leave of the Cleveland Way, which turns sharply to follow the old road north, while we continue to take advantage of the trackbed for no less than five miles further, contouring around the head of Farndale and its many infant streams.

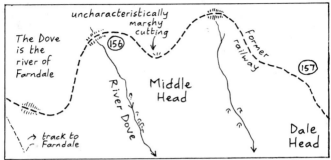

The Dove is the river of Farndale

uncharacteristically marshy cutting

(156)

former railway

(157)

River Dove

Middle Head

Dale Head

→ track to Farndale

From Bloworth Crossing to beneath the Lion Inn on Blakey Ridge, we follow the track-bed of the ROSEDALE IRONSTONE RAILWAY, built in 1861 to convey ironstone from Rosedale, in the heart of the moors, out over the watershed and down to the furnaces of Tees-side. This remarkable feat of engineering saw trains cross the moors at 1300ft. With the demise of the industry the line closed in 1929, and today it is difficult to visualise either the trains or the thousands labouring hard in now tranquil Rosedale.

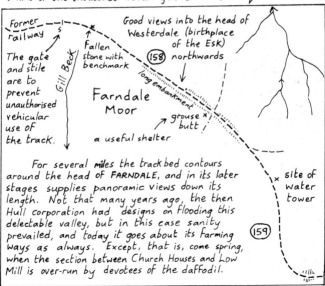

Former railway

The gate and stile are to prevent unauthorised vehicular use of the track.

Gill Beck

Fallen stone with benchmark

Good views into the head of Westerdale (birthplace of the Esk)

(158) northwards

long embankment

Farndale Moor

grouse butt

a useful shelter

site of water tower

(159)

For several miles the track bed contours around the head of FARNDALE, and in its later stages supplies panoramic views down its length. Not that many years ago, the then Hull corporation had designs on flooding this delectable valley, but in this case sanity prevailed, and today it goes about its farming ways as always. Except, that is, come spring, when the section between Church Houses and Low Mill is over-run by devotees of the daffodil.

At a final cutting the *Lion Inn* at Blakey appears inspiringly on the skyline ahead, and the head of one last side-valley is rounded before a clear path strikes off left to climb through the heather up to a wallside and the standing stone on Blakey Howe, immediately above the hostelry. Beyond the moor road is the head of Rosedale, and while the rail track heads that way, it does so without us. Few will resist a break at the *Lion,* a rare opportunity for en route refreshment.

On emerging blinking into the daylight, turn north along the capacious verge for a mile as far as a large, ungainly stone on the left known as Margery Bradley. A path now strikes off to the right through heather, cutting the corner of the road junction at Rosedale Head to meet the Rosedale Abbey road at the prominent guide of White Cross.

THE LION INN dates back over 400 years, and while it was once frequented by ironstone and coal miners, today it is a prominent landmark waylaying most of the walkers and tourists who pass by. The highway it services carries a surprising volume of traffic considering it is a humble moor road: the answer lies in it being an ideal link - with little competition for many a mile - between villages in the north and south of the Park, without severe gradients or corners.

South of the Lion is Blakey Junction, where the former railway divided for either Rosedale West Mines, or to encircle Rosedale Head for several miles more to Rosedale East Mines.

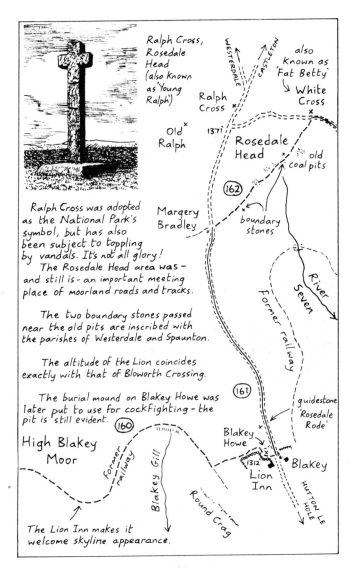

Ralph Cross, Rosedale Head (also known as 'Young Ralph')

WESTERDALE

CASTLETON

also known as 'Fat Betty'

White Cross

Ralph Cross ×

Old × Ralph

1371

Rosedale Head

old coal pits

162

boundary stones

River Seven

Margery Bradley

Ralph Cross was adopted as the National Park's symbol, but has also been subject to toppling by vandals. It's not all glory!

The Rosedale Head area was – and still is – an important meeting place of moorland roads and tracks.

The two boundary stones passed near the old pits are inscribed with the parishes of Westerdale and Spaunton.

The altitude of the Lion coincides exactly with that of Bloworth Crossing.

The burial mound on Blakey Howe was later put to use for cockfighting – the pit is still evident.

Former railway

161

guidestone 'Rosedale Rode'

160

High Blakey Moor

Former railway

Blakey Gill

Blakey Howe

1312

Lion Inn

Blakey

HUTTON LE HOLE

Round Crag

The Lion Inn makes its welcome skyline appearance.

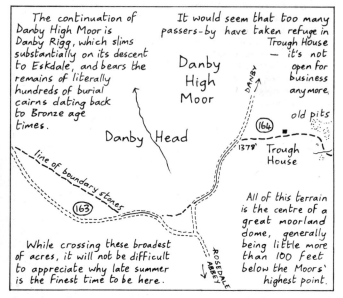

The continuation of Danby High Moor is Danby Rigg, which slims substantially on its descent to Eskdale, and bears the remains of literally hundreds of burial cairns dating back to Bronze age times.

It would seem that too many passers-by have taken refuge in Trough House — it's not open for business anymore.

Danby High Moor

DANBY

old pits

164

1378' Trough House

Danby Head

line of boundary stones

163

All of this terrain is the centre of a great moorland dome, generally being little more than 100 feet below the Moors' highest point.

While crossing these broadest of acres, it will not be difficult to appreciate why late summer is the finest time to be here.

ROSEDALE ABBEY

Go right a short way and then short-cut the road again on a path forking left to trace a chain of boundary stones. Back on the road for only a minute or so, yet another corner is cut by a thin but clear path that emerges on the single-track road branching down to the left for Little Fryup Dale. This is accompanied over a gentle brow with Eskdale outspread far ahead, and as Trough House appears, a broad track soon branches off for it. Beyond the padlocked stone shooting hut the path encounters the head-waters of Great Fryup Beck, there encircling in grand style the head of Great Fryup Dale.

This is a splendid section, the heather surrounds of many miles being enhanced by the addition of bilberry and (hopefully in moderation) bracken, while the colourful and rough-fashioned dalehead drops steeply away to the left. Continuing on the broad path eventually filters onto a moorland road. Turn left as far as a broad track branching straight ahead as the road swings left to a white Ordnance column.

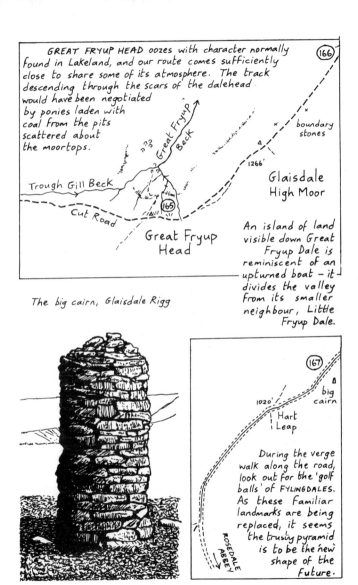

GREAT FRYUP HEAD oozes with character normally found in Lakeland, and our route comes sufficiently close to share some of its atmosphere. The track descending through the scars of the dalehead would have been negotiated by ponies laden with coal from the pits scattered about the moortops.

Great Fryup Beck

boundary stones

Trough Gill Beck

1266'

Glaisdale High Moor

Cut Road

165

Great Fryup Head

An island of land visible down Great Fryup Dale is reminiscent of an upturned boat – it divides the valley from its smaller neighbour, Little Fryup Dale.

The big cairn, Glaisdale Rigg

167

1020'

big cairn

Hart Leap

During the verge walk along the road, look out for the 'golf balls' of FYLINGDALES. As these familiar landmarks are being replaced, it seems the trusty pyramid is to be the new shape of the future.

ROSEDALE ABBEY

125

This is the old road along Glaisdale Rigg, and is followed unerringly all the way down to its village, a super promenade regardless of the time and one's condition. Heather moor gives way to grass moor as height is lost, with the Eskdale scene increasing in clarity correspondingly. Eventually the old road meets a surfaced lanehead to drop down onto the green at the head of Glaisdale.

There are several permutations of route from here to the railway station at the village foot, and these may depend upon the location of one's chosen lodging, if any. All steps first turn right, the direct route adhering to the main road that swings gracefully down to the station at Beggar's Bridge. Alternatively turn down a snicket above the terrace containing the post office, and at the bottom follow a quieter road back along the dale floor; or stay on the road as far as the *Mitre,* and then strike left down a narrow road. All lead to the neighbourhood of Beggar's Bridge.

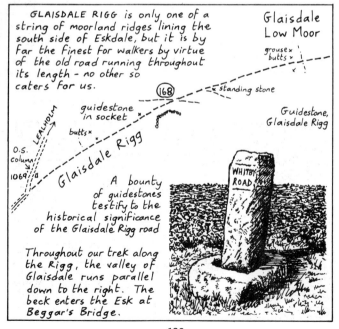

GLAISDALE RIGG is only one of a string of moorland ridges lining the south side of Eskdale, but it is by far the finest for walkers by virtue of the old road running throughout its length - no other so caters for us.

Glaisdale Low Moor

grouse× butts×

(168)

standing stone

guidestone in socket

Guidestone, Glaisdale Rigg

LEALHOLM

butts×

O.S. column

1069

Glaisdale Rigg

WHITBY ROAD

A bounty of guidestones testify to the historical significance of the Glaisdale Rigg road

Throughout our trek along the Rigg, the valley of Glaisdale runs parallel down to the right. The beck enters the Esk at Beggar's Bridge.

GLAISDALE is a scattered village comprising of three distinct corners spreading from the inurned environs of Beggar's Bridge up to the very edge of breezy Glaisdale Rigg. At the foot of its own substantial side-valley, it boasts both lovely woods and rolling moors on its doorstep, and typifies the Esk Valley in its commendable attempts to deter the motor car from making logical progress: truly the railway is a necessity here. Peaceful today, Glaisdale was caught up in the 19th century iron ore 'boom' - when mining was in full swing one of its three hostelries underwent a name change to the 'Three Blast Furnaces', which were actually operating nearby.

LEALHOLM

Esk Valley Line

River Esk

Glaisdale Hall Farm

(170)

(169)

GLAISDALE HEAD

Glaisdale

This prominent embankment belongs to a long departed tramway to a former ironstone mine.

Beggar's Bridge, Glaisdale

127

SECTION 12
GLAISDALE TO ROBIN HOOD'S BAY
20 miles   *1700 feet of ascent*

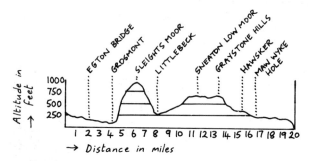

This final stage is an extravaganza of variety, comprising old toll road, steam trains, burial mounds, several tracts of heather moor, an idyllic hamlet, a beautiful waterfall in glorious woodland, and last but not least, an exhilarating clifftop.

The only snag with this glorious finale is its length: by now you'll either be struggling gamely on to the end, or in condition to face up to Everest. If the former, then the prospect of crawling into Robin Hood's Bay as the sun sets, in no condition to undertake the ritual celebrations, will be sufficient to wish you'd planned a shorter last lap. This is best achieved by starting from Grosmont (see page 12).

The wayward lurching of the route, however, is such that if you've bitten off too much, there are at least opportunities to omit sections - the shame is that none deserve such treatment. Anyway, here are the options. Take an old pannier way from Grosmont along the valley side to Sleights, and if desperate cling to the valley floor to taste salt-water at Whitby, or cross from Sleights to Sneaton and pick up the route at Hawsker. Two easier finishes are a direct march from Graystone Hills, or a brisk walk along the old railway instead of the clifftop (this saves little). In totally different vein, consider heading north from Glaisdale to pick an interesting route to a finish at Staithes, similarly appointed to Robin Hood's Bay but less crowded.

At the railway station, Beggar's Bridge is hidden behind the long, low railway viaduct: pass under it to view the old pack bridge and then return to leave the road immediately by a footbridge over Glaisdale Beck to enter East Arnecliff Wood. The path climbs steeply, nears the river, and soon climbs again on a prolonged paved section. A gentler conclusion leads out onto a quiet road: turn down the hill towards Egton Bridge.

BEGGAR'S BRIDGE is a work of art, a graceful arched structure high above the Esk. The present bridge dates from the early 1600s, and served the packhorse era. It is said to have originally been built by Tom Ferris, a local lad who became Mayor of Hull. Now a tourist attraction, it is sat incongruously between a dark railway bridge and a modern, featureless road bridge.

The path through EAST ARNECLIFF WOOD (above) traces the course of a centuries-old pannier-way, one of many such trade-routes that criss-cross Eskdale. Though packhorse days may be long gone, they still serve modern travellers.

First encountered at Beggar's Bridge, and sharing a similar valley-bottom course as far as Grosmont, is the ESK VALLEY LINE. A miracle survivor of Beeching's axe, this railway bears the hallmark of a rural line of several decades past. More importantly, the Middlesbrough-Whitby railway is a lifeline to the communities along its route, for the valley does not readily take to buses. Chasing the Esk through the winding dale floor, it bridges the river on no less than 18 occasions.

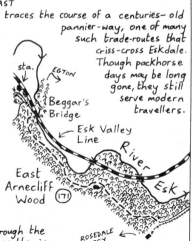

sta.
EGTON
Beggar's Bridge
Esk Valley Line
River Esk
East Arnecliff Wood (171)
ROSEDALE ABBEY
Delves

At a T-junction just past the *Horseshoe* the way keeps on to the road bridge over the Esk, but a more attractive option is to go down some steps to the river, where dependable stepping-stones cross it. Up onto the road, turn right to a junction between the church and the road bridge (Egton Bridge itself).

Depart Egton Bridge by the enclosed way almost opposite, signposted 'Egton Estates - private road'. Early on be sure to glance back to see Egton Manor, noting the ha-ha which keeps animals off the lawn without jarring the view. This former toll road runs along the valley floor of the Esk - passing a surviving notice of tolls - to emerge onto a road on the edge of Grosmont.

Turn right over the sturdy bridge to enter the village, along to the level crossing in the centre. Departure is simply by going straight on up the street climbing out, ignoring two branches left (both for Whitby via Sleights).

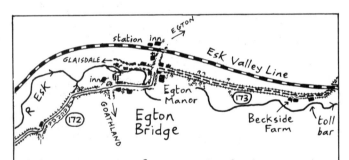

EGTON BRIDGE is a fascinating place for its size, rich in historical, natural and cultural attractions. Neighbour of the hilltop Egton village, it stands embowered in greenery in a particularly lovely corner of Eskdale. This was the birthplace of Nicholas Postgate, 'martyr of the moors'. After training in France he spent many post-Reformation decades working in this strongly Catholic district. Finally apprehended in 1679, he was hung, drawn and quartered for his 'crimes', on the Knavesmire at York, an old priest of 82.

His memory is perpetuated by a village inn, and his faith by the beautiful church of St. Hedda, built in 1866 and famed for its detailed bas-relief panels set into the exterior walls depicting scenes from the life of Christ.

GROSMONT is a pleasant enough village, firmly embedded at the foot of numerous steep roads. Dominated in the 19th century by ironstone mining (of which the scars remain) there is less to see of earlier times, when – then as Grosmont – it supported an abbey of the little known Grantimontine Order. Dissolved in 1536, Priory Farm now occupies the site. Earlier still, a Roman Fort existed in the neighbourhood.

Today railways take centre stage in Grosmont, for British Rail's Esk Valley Line meets the privately operated North Yorkshire Moors Railway here, each having its own station. The Whitby – Pickering Railway opened in 1836 as a horse-drawn tramway, and a decade later was improved to take locomotives. The section south of Grosmont was closed in 1965, only to be saved by enthusiasts and re-opened (initially to Goathland) in 1973. Today visitors can enjoy a steam-hauled 18 miles run to Pickering through the very heart of the moors – a memorable trip.

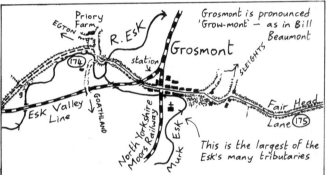

Grosmont is pronounced 'Grow-mont' – as in Bill Beaumont

This is the largest of the Esk's many tributaries

Further interest at Egton Bridge is found in its annual Gooseberry Show, held every August for 2 centuries. The toll road is another tradition – though the charges no longer apply.

Always, at Egton Bridge, there is of course the Esk itself, a famous salmon river and the National Park's major watercourse. Its journey from the moors to Whitby is one worth the following.

Surviving notice on the old toll road

BARNARDS ROAD TOLL		
1 HORSE 2 WHEELS		4ᵈ
2 " " "		8ᵈ
1 " 4 "		8ᵈ
2 " " "		1ᶜ
3 " " "		1ᶜ
MOTOR CAR 4 "		1ᶜ
" 3 "		1ᶜ
MOTOR CYCLE SIDE CAR		1ᶜ
MOTOR LORRY		2ᶜ
MOTOR BUS		3ᶜ
TRACTOR		1ᶜ
HEARSE		6ᵈ
THIS GATE IS CLOSED AND LOCKED AT 10 PM DAILY		
EGTON ESTATES OFFICE AUG 1948		

Above: Littlebeck

Though extensively damaged now, the BRIDE STONES were originally circles at least 30 feet in diameter.

FLAT HOWE is a round barrow in a kerb of retaining stones – heather enthusiastically covers it. Arousing greater enthusiasm to us, however, is the wide sweep of coastline in view. Whitby is revealed in near-entirety – it's a long time since we were near anywhere that size. Coincidentally enough, its relationship with Robin Hood's Bay is not dissimilar to that between Whitehaven and St Bees. Remember St Bees?

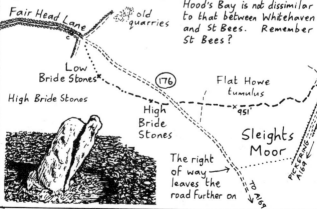

Fair Head Lane

old quarries

Low Bride Stones

High Bride Stones

(176)

Flat Howe tumulus

951

High Bride Stones

Sleights Moor

PICKERING A169

The right of way leaves the road further on

to A169

The road (Fair Head Lane) is a right old pull, enlivened by the retrospective views over Eskdale to the moors above, and more significantly, a good seascape at the foot of Eskdale, where Whitby Abbey claims prominence on its clifftop site. When the road breaks onto the open moor its surface can be escaped by slanting slightly right to locate the line of standing stones known as Low Bride Stones, skulking in a reedy patch of ground. From them rise parallel to the road, a thin path in parts might be located as a level walk ensues to the more open aspect of High Bride Stones: these are fewer but more conspicuous. Here slant back across to the road, and there cross straight over onto a thin but well-defined path heading through heather up to the mound of Flat Howe on the crest of Sleights Moor.

Having absorbed the panorama, head now for the much nearer wooded valley of Little Beck. A path winds down to the left before meeting the broad highway of the A169 at the top of Blue Bank. A stile admits to its verge, and a few yards up the opposite verge another stile sees a bridlepath strike down the moor, eventually leaving the heather for bracken: at the bottom a stony track is joined for the final yards down the head of a surfaced lane. Continue down, joining a through road to maintain this direct descent into the sylvan setting of the hamlet of Littlebeck.

Over either footbridge or ford climb the road as far as the second bend, where a wicket-gate on the right leads into the woods. A good path heads upstream, becoming temporarily diverted from Little Beck by a waterfall on a small tributary.

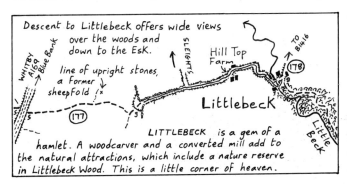

Descent to Littlebeck offers wide views over the woods and down to the Esk.

WHITBY A169 Blue Bank

line of upright stones, a former sheepfold

SLEIGHTS

Hill Top Farm

TO B1416

178

Littlebeck

177

Little Beck

LITTLEBECK is a gem of a hamlet. A woodcarver and a converted mill add to the natural attractions, which include a nature reserve in Littlebeck Wood. This is a little corner of heaven.

133

Falling Foss

After a climb over a spoil heap continue on, before climbing steeply to the Hermitage. Leave by the upper path, and when this forks take the right branch down to Falling Foss, arriving at a well-sited viewpoint above the falls. From the nearby footbridge take the path up to cross a farm road and continue upstream. Within a minute the path fords the beck, though if impassable one could return to cross the farm road bridge and, just above it, take a path above the opposite bank. The path improves to lead up to the car park and bridge at May Beck.

Turn up the road doubling back left, and just past the sharp bend above New May Beck Farm a broad path strikes off across Sneaton Low Moor. Though it thins markedly it remains clear, to join the B1416. Turning right, a well-tramped Coast-to-Coasters' verge aids progress.

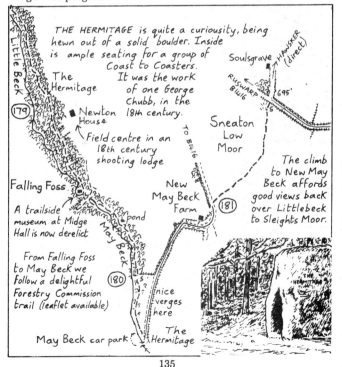

THE HERMITAGE is quite a curiousity, being hewn out of a solid boulder. Inside is ample seating for a group of Coast to Coasters.
It was the work of one George Chubb, in the 18th century.

Little Beck

The Hermitage

(179)

Newton House

Field centre in an 18th century shooting lodge

Falling Foss

A trailside museum at Midge Hall is now derelict

pond

From Falling Foss to May Beck we follow a delightful Forestry Commission trail (leaflet available)

(180)

May Beck

May Beck car park

The Hermitage

Soulsgrave

HAWSKER (direct)

RUSWARP B1416

695'

Sneaton Low Moor

to B1416

New May Beck Farm

(181)

The climb to New May Beck affords good views back over Littlebeck to Sleights Moor.

nice verges here

THE HERMITAGE

135

A constant procession of Coast to Coasters has forged a clear path across previously trackless GRAYSTONE HILLS. A modest-width trod ensures we can enjoy our final commune with the uplands, even if a little tired. Ahead, Whitby lures us ever onwards towards the coastline.

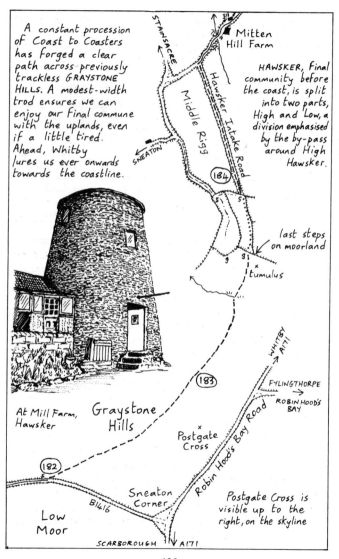

STAINSACRE

Mitten Hill Farm

HAWSKER, Final community before the coast, is split into two parts, High and Low, a division emphasised by the by-pass around High Hawsker.

Middle Rigg

Hawsker Intake Road

SNEATON

184

5 5

last steps on moorland

9 9

x tumulus

WHITBY A171

FYLINGTHORPE

ROBIN HOOD'S BAY

183

At Mill Farm, Hawsker

Graystone Hills

x Postgate Cross

Robin Hood's Bay Road

182

B1416

Sneaton Corner

Low Moor

SCARBOROUGH   A171

Postgate Cross is visible up to the right, on the skyline

136

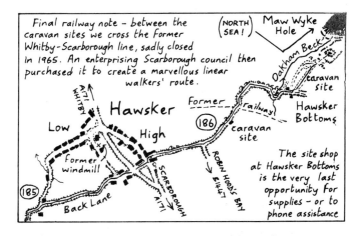

Final railway note – between the caravan sites we cross the former Whitby–Scarborough line, sadly closed in 1965. An enterprising Scarborough council then purchased it to create a marvellous linear walkers' route.

(NORTH SEA!)

Maw Wyke Hole

Oakham Beck

caravan site

Hawsker Bottoms

Hawsker

Former railway

Low

High

186

caravan site

A171 WHITBY

Former Windmill

185

Back Lane

SCARBOROUGH A171

ROBIN HOOD'S BAY B1447

The site shop at Hawsker Bottoms is the very last opportunity for supplies – or to phone assistance

Before too long a stile on the other side of the road gives access to the great heathery tracts of Graystone Hills. With a seascape ahead again, another thin, clear path heads away for a magic stroll away from the busy A171 over to the right. Happily this road is avoided as the path swings further north to cling tenaciously to our final march of heather. Just left of a tumulus a gate sees us off the moor for good, and the path duly disappears. Just over the brow of the field the red roofs of Hawsker appear, and the way descends the right side of the field to a stile into the head of Hawsker Intake Road. This leafy byway opens into a wider track to descend to a quiet back road, turning right for the village. The main A171 road is a final obstacle before entering the village street.

Continue out along the road to Robin Hood's Bay, and when it swings right keep straight on, past one caravan site and down to a second one. Just past the site shop the road ends, and here descend the site road through the caravans, continuing down as a path takes over to meet the coast path above Maw Wyke Hole, and thus, after a long absence, the Cleveland Way. This is indeed a classic moment: reaching the coast is sufficiently thrilling but the grandeur of the scenery makes it doubly satisfying. Turn right to savour the final miles.

The way ahead is distinctly obvious as it is bounded on one side by majestic cliffs and thence the North Sea. On eventually rounding Ness Point beneath a coastguard lookout, Robin Hood's Bay comes fully into view, and the village itself is soon within our sights. At last a wicket-gate leads into trees to emerge onto a residential street, Mount Pleasant North. At the end turn left to descend the bustling main street all the way down through the heart of the village to its inevitable conclusion. Keep on out onto the stony shore, just as far as the North Sea happens to be, and that's it, you've done it!

ROBIN HOOD'S BAY, with the advantages of an exciting name and an even better location, will be found in many people's list of favourite places. Once the quiet preserve of fishermen and smugglers, it is now very much part of the tourist itinerary.

Known in the locality simply as Bay Town, it consists of a chaotic tumble of red-roofed buildings squeezed into a narrow break in the cliffs. From the modern extension on the clifftop, the steep main street plunges down to the very sea. On each side are irregular groupings of shops and dwellings, with narrow passageways linking the near-hidden doorsteps.

Over the years the village has suffered greatly from storms, and the savage waters once drove a ship into the Bay Hotel: a modern sea-wall now ensures rather more safety. The bay itself is regarded as a geologists' mecca, with fossils and eager school parties in abundance.

Boggle Hole youth hostel

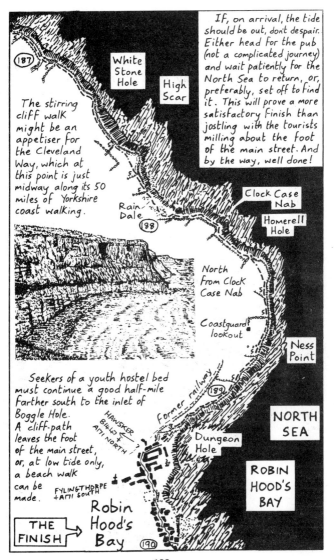

If, on arrival, the tide should be out, don't despair. Either head for the pub (not a complicated journey) and wait patiently for the North Sea to return, or, preferably, set off to find it. This will prove a more satisfactory finish than jostling with the tourists milling about the foot of the main street. And by the way, well done!

White Stone Hole

High Scar

The stirring cliff walk might be an appetiser for the Cleveland Way, which at this point is just midway along its 50 miles of Yorkshire coast walking.

Rain Dale

Clock Case Nab

Homerell Hole

North From Clock Case Nab

Coastguard lookout

Ness Point

Seekers of a youth hostel bed must continue a good half-mile farther south to the inlet of Boggle Hole. A cliff-path leaves the foot of the main street, or, at low tide only, a beach walk can be made.

Former railway

HAWSKER B.446 + A171 NORTH

NORTH SEA

Dungeon Hole

ROBIN HOOD'S BAY

FYLINGTHORPE + A171 SOUTH

Robin Hood's Bay

THE FINISH

139

RECORD OF THE JOURNEY

Date (LEFT)	Place	Miles daily	Miles total	Notes
15.5.92	St Bees	-	-	
15.5.92	Sandwith	4½	4½	
	Cleator	8½	8½	
	Dent	10½	10½	
	Ennerdale Bridge	14	14	
	Gillerthwaite	5	19	
14.5.92	Black Sail Hut	9	23	
	Honister Pass	11½	25½	
	Seatoller	13¼	27¼	
	Rosthwaite	14½	28½	
	Stonethwaite	1	29½	
	Greenup Edge	3¾	32¼	
13.5.92	Easedale	8	36½	
	Grasmere	9	37½	
	Grisedale Hause	12½	41	
12.5.92	Patterdale	17½	46	
	Boredale Hause	1	47	
	Kidsty Pike	5	51	
	Haweswater	6¾	52¾	
	Burnbanks	11	57	
	Rosgill Bridge	13	59	
11.5.92	Shap	16	62	
	Oddendale	3	65	
	Orton	8¼	70¼	
	Sunbiggin Tarn	12	74	
	Smardale Bridge	16	78	
	Waitby junction	18	80	
10.5.92	Kirkby Stephen	20	82	
	Hartley	1	83	
	9 Standards Rigg	5½	87½	
	Raven Seat	10¼	92¼	
9.5.92	Keld	13	95	

Date (LEFT)	Place	Miles daily	total	Notes
	Gunnerside Gill	$3^{1}/_{2}$	$98^{1}/_{2}$	
	Surrender Bridge	$7^{1}/_{2}$	$102^{1}/_{2}$	
	Reeth	11	106	
8.5.92	Grinton	$1^{1}/_{4}$	$107^{1}/_{4}$	
	Marrick	$3^{3}/_{4}$	$109^{3}/_{4}$	
	Marske	$6^{1}/_{4}$	$112^{1}/_{4}$	
	Richmond	11	117	
	Colburn	3	120	
7.5.92	Catterick Bridge	$5^{3}/_{4}$	$122^{3}/_{4}$	BROMPTON-ON-SWALE
	Bolton on Swale	$7^{1}/_{2}$	$124^{1}/_{2}$	
	Danby Wiske	14	131	
	Oaktree Hill	16	133	
	Long Lane	$18^{1}/_{2}$	$135^{1}/_{2}$	
	A19	22	139	
6.5.92	Ingleby Cross	23	140	
	Beacon Hill	2	142	
	Huthwaite Green	5	145	
	Carlton Bank	8	148	
	The Wainstones	$10^{3}/_{4}$	$150^{3}/_{4}$	
	Clay Bank Top	12	152	
	Round Hill	$1^{3}/_{4}$	$153^{3}/_{4}$	
	Bloworth Crossing	$3^{1}/_{4}$	$155^{1}/_{4}$	
5.5.92	Lion, Blakey	$8^{3}/_{4}$	$160^{3}/_{4}$	
	Trough House	12	164	
	Glaisdale	18	170	
	Beggar's Bridge	$^{1}/_{2}$	$170^{1}/_{2}$	
	Egton Bridge	$2^{1}/_{2}$	$172^{1}/_{2}$	
	Grosmont	$4^{1}/_{2}$	$174^{1}/_{2}$	
	Littlebeck	8	178	
	New May Beck	11	181	
	Hawsker	$15^{1}/_{2}$	$185^{1}/_{2}$	
4.5.92 / 3.5.92	Robin Hood's Bay	20	190	

RECORD OF ACCOMMODATION

Date	Address	Notes
3.5.92	THE STUDIO, THORPE LANE ROBIN HOOD'S BAY	
4.5.92	THE LION INN BLAKEY	
5.5.92	N. YORK MOORS OUTDOOR CENTRE, INGLEBY CROSS	
6.5.92	'THE OAST HOUSE' BROMPTON-ON-SWALE	
7.5.92	GRINTON LODGE Y.H.A.	
8.5.92	KELD YHA.	
9.5.92	KIRKBY STEPHEN BLACK BULL	
10.5.92	SHAP 'PLEASANT VIEW'	
11.5.92	PATTERDALE Y.H.A.	
12.5.92	THORNEY HOW Y.H.A, GRASMERE	
13.5.92	BLACK SAIL Y.H.A.	
14.5.92	SANDWITH MRS. DAY	

RECORD OF INNS VISITED

Name	Location	Notes
BAY HOTEL	ROBIN HOODS BAY	
THE LAUREL	" "	
THE VICTORIA	" "	
LION INN	BLAKEY MOOR	
WHITE SWAN	DANBY WISKE	
THE CROWN	BROMPTON-ON-SWALE	
KING WILLIAM THE IV	BROMPTON-ON-SWALE	
BLACK BULL	KIRKBY STEPHEN	
KING'S ARMS	KIRKBY STEPHEN	
THE GEORGE	ORTON	
THE GREYHOUND	SHAP	
TRAVELLER'S REST	GRASMERE	
FOX + HOUNDS	ENNERDALE BRIDGE	
DOG + PARTRIDGE	SANDWITH	
QUEEN'S HOTEL	ST. BEES	

INDEX

Place names on the route maps

INDEX continued

INDEX continued

INDEX continued

INDEX continued

INDEX continued

HILLSIDE GUIDES

LONG DISTANCE WALKS - LAKE DISTRICT

1 * **THE WESTMORLAND WAY** Appleby to Arnside
2 * **THE FURNESS WAY** Arnside to Ravenglass
3 * **THE CUMBERLAND WAY** Ravenglass to Appleby

LONG DISTANCE WALKS - NORTHERN ENGLAND

7 * **CLEVELAND WAY COMPANION** Helmsley to Filey
9 * **NORTH BOWLAND TRAVERSE** Slaidburn to
Stainforth (by David Johnson)
16 * **DALES WAY COMPANION** Ilkley to Bowness
22 * **THE COAST TO COAST WALK** St Bees to Robin
Hood's Bay

CIRCULAR WALKS - YORKSHIRE DALES

4 * **WALKS IN WHARFEDALE**
20 * **RAMBLES IN WHARFEDALE**
5 * **WALKS IN NIDDERDALE**
6 * **WALKS IN THE CRAVEN DALES**
8 * **WALKS IN WENSLEYDALE**
10 * **WALKS IN THREE PEAKS COUNTRY**
11 * **WALKS IN SWALEDALE**
21 * **WALKS ON THE HOWGILL FELLS**

CIRCULAR WALKS - NORTH YORK MOORS

CIRCULAR WALKS - SOUTH PENNINES

HILLWALKING - THE LAKE DISTRICT

FREEDOM OF THE DALES
40 Selected Walks
Full colour hardback

By the same author, published by Cordee, Leicester:

80 DALES WALKS - A hardback omnibus edition of
Books 4, 6, 8, 10 and 11.

Honister Crag